THE GREEK ISLANDS
Genius Loci

View of Naxos island seen through the monumental doorway of the Archaic temple.
Thomas Hope (1769-1831)   Watercolour, 44 x 29 cm.   Benaki Museum, Inv. No. 27375.

Author's acknowledgements

This series of twenty books covering the Aegean Islands is the fruit of many years of solitary dedication to a job difficult to accomplish given the extent of the subject matter and the geography involved. My belief throughout has been that only what is seen with the eyes can trustfully be written about; and to that end I have attempted to walk, ride, drive, climb, sail and swim these Islands in order to inspect everything talked about here. There will be errors in this text inevitably for which, although working in good faith, I alone am responsible. Notwithstanding, I am confident that these are the best, most clearly explanatory and most comprehensive artistic accounts currently available of this vibrant and historically dense corner of the Mediterranean.

Professor Robin Barber, author of the last, general, *Blue Guide to Greece* (based in turn on Stuart Rossiter's masterful text of the 1960s), has been very generous with support and help; and I am also particularly indebted to Charles Arnold for meticulously researched factual data on the Islands and for his support throughout this project. I could not have asked for a more saintly and helpful editor, corrector and indexer than Judy Tither. Efi Stathopoulou, Peter Cocconi, Marc René de Montalembert, Valentina Ivancich, William Forrester and Geoffrey Cox have all given invaluable help; and I owe a large debt of gratitude to John and Jay Rendall for serial hospitality and encouragement. For companionship on many journeys, I would like to thank a number of dear friends: Graziella Seferiades, Ivan Tabares, Matthew Kidd, Martin Leon, my group of Louisianan friends, and my brother Iain— all of whose different reactions to and passions for Greece have been a constant inspiration.

This work is dedicated with admiration and deep affection to Ivan de Jesus Tabares-Valencia who, though a native of the distant Andes mountains, from the start understood the profound spiritual appeal of the Aegean world.

McGILCHRIST'S GREEK ISLANDS

20. SOUTHERN CYCLADES
AMORGOS, IOS, SIKINOS &
FOLEGANDROS

GENIUS LOCI PUBLICATIONS
London

McGilchrist's Greek Islands 20. Southern Cyclades
First edition

Published by Genius Loci Publications
54 Eccleston Road, London W13 0RL

Nigel McGilchrist © 2010
Nigel McGilchrist has asserted his moral rights.

ISBN 978-1-907859-14-4

A CIP catalogue record of this book is available from the British Library.

The author and publisher cannot accept responsibility or liability for
information contained herein, this being in some cases difficult to verify
and subject to change.

Layout and copy-editing by Judy Tither

Cover design by Kate Buckle

Maps and plans by Nick Hill Design

Printed and bound in Great Britain by TJ International Ltd, Padstow, Cornwall

The island maps in this series are based on the cartography of
Terrain Maps
Karneadou 4, 106 75 Athens, Greece
T: +30 210 609 5759, Fx: +30 210 609 5859
terrain@terrainmaps.gr
www.terrainmaps.gr

This book is one of twenty which comprise the complete, detailed
manuscript which the author prepared for the *Blue Guide: Greece,
the Aegean Islands* (2010), and on which the *Blue Guide* was
based. Some of this text therefore appears in the *Blue Guide*.

A NOTE ON THE TEXT & MAPS

Some items in the text are marked with an asterisk: these may be monuments, landscapes, curiosities or individual artefacts and works of art. The asterisk is not simply an indication of the renown of a particular place or item, but is intended to draw the reader's attention to things that have a uniquely interesting quality or are of particular beauty.

A small number of hotels and eateries are also marked with asterisks in the *Practical Information* sections, implying that their quality or their setting is notably special. These books do not set out to be guides to lodging and eating in the Islands, and our recommendations here are just an attempt to help with a few suggestions for places that have been selected with an eye to simplicity and unpretentiousness. We believe they may be the kind of places that a reader of this book would be seeking and would enjoy.

On the island maps:

⁂ denotes a site with visible prehistoric or ancient remains

✝ denotes a church referred to in the text
(on Island Maps only rural churches are marked)

✝ denotes a monastery, convent or large church referred to in the text

⊡ denotes a Byzantine or Mediaeval castle

� denotes an ancient stone tower

⛲ denotes an important fresh-water or geothermic spring

⛴ denotes a harbour with connecting ferry services

Road and path networks:

- a continuous line denotes a metalled road or unsurfaced track feasible for motors

- a dotted line denotes footpath only

CONTENTS

Amorgos   **9**

Ios   **59**

Sikinos   **85**

Folegandros   **107**

Glossary   **125**

Index   **129**

Maps
  Amorgos   8
  Ios   58
  Sikinos   84
  Folegandros   106

Plans
  Katapola Bay area   18
  Ancient *Minoa*   19
  Amorgos Chora   26
  Folegandros Chora   111

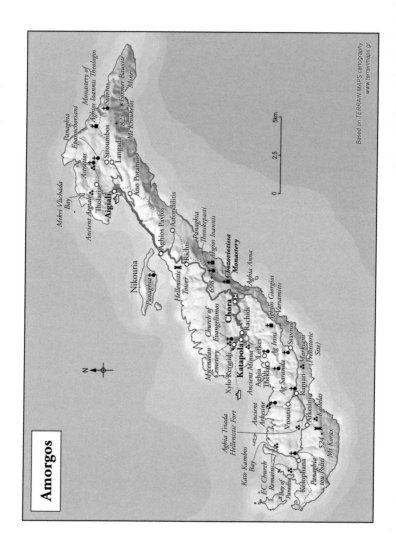

Amorgos

N

Based on TERRAIN MAPS cartography
www.terrainmaps.gr

0   2.5   5km

Monastery of
Aghios Ioannis Theologos
Former Bauxite
Mines
Mt Krikelos 823
Stavros
Panaghia
Epanochoriani
Langada
Astratios
Stroumbos
Tholaria
Ano Potamos
Ancient Aegiale
Aigiali
Miki Vlichada
Bay
Aghios Pavlos
Astondilitis
Richti
Panaghia
Theoskepasti
Aghios Ioannis
Nikouria
Hellenistic
Tower
698
Chozoviotissa
Monastery
Panaghia
Aghia Anna
Mycenaean
Cemetery
Church of
Evangelismos
Chora
Rachidi
Aghios Giorgios
Varsamitis
Xylo-Keraidi
Katapola
Lefkes
Ag Irinis
Stavros
Ancient Minoa
Aghia
Triada
Ag Saranda
Kamari
Markiani
(Prehistoric
Site)
Ancient
Arkesini
Vroutsi
Arkesini
Aghia Triada
Hellenistic Fort
Kato Kambos
Bay
Mt Korax 524
Kolophana
Kaïtelas
EC Church
Remains
Bay of
Panaghia
Panaghia
tou Politi

AMORGOS

The grand landscapes of Amorgós are full of dramatic settings. A long human presence on the island has left many monuments and settlements behind, all of them characterised by sites of courageous beauty. When the island was an important centre of Cycladic culture in the 3rd millennium BC, trading with Naxos and the smaller islands in its own protective lea and producing marble sculpture of the highest quality, the citadel at Markianí was built on a cliff-top summit looking across open waters to Thera in the south and to Naxos in the north. Nearly 2,000 years later, the three cities founded in historic times on Amorgos—tactfully distanced from one another so as to divide the island into three equal parts—all occupy exhilarating summits or promontories. And 2,000 years later again, when monks fleeing Arab incursions into Palestine took refuge on the island, they established their community in the most improbable site of all, half-way up a 400m precipice above the sea. The famous monastery of the Panaghia Chozoviótissa which grew from this community is one the most unforgettable sites of the Aegean. It was visited by le Corbusier in 1933 and notably influenced his work.

The quality of the archaeological remains is often as

remarkable as the setting. The fortified refuge-tower or complex of farm-buildings at Aghia Triada near Arkesíni is the most impressive of any which has come down to us from Hellenistic times, both in its dimensions and in the quality of its construction. And from the same epoch, even the lowly lavatories of the ancient *gymnasium* at *Minoa*—roof, seats and flushing drain still intact—must surely be the best preserved conveniences from Greek Antiquity anywhere.

Few other islands combine as succinctly so much history and landscape and important archaeology as Amorgos: and few do it with such disarming simplicity. A little modernity has come to the island in roads and buildings and tourism, but never obtrusively. The two ports of the island, the Chora, and the villages of the rural interior, have all been well preserved without any straining pretension, and development on Amorgos has remained respectful of the island's history and dignified grandeur. Walking on the island is a great pleasure, too. The paths—many of them ancient arteries of communication—are well marked. Both the more agrarian plateaux of western Amorgos and the dramatic, Hebridean slopes of the eastern end of the island, leave deep impressions in the memory for the beauty of their vegetation and the splendid views which they afford.

HISTORY

Settlement began on Amorgos in the late 5th millennium BC at the hill-top of Minoa where obsidian from Milos and Late Neolithic clay vessels have been found. The 3rd millennium BC marks the island's first apogee, when it was an important centre of the Cycladic culture which flourished contemporaneously on Naxos and in the islands of the protected waters in between. Amorgos, with almost a dozen separate inhabited centres in this period, is the origin of many famous Cycladic figurines and of the idiosyncratic 'Dokathismata style'. Cemeteries at Aghia Paraskevi, Aghios Pavlos, Dokathismata, Kapros, Kapsala, Nikouriá and Stavrós have all yielded Cycladic sculpture. From the 2nd millennium BC, apart from evidence of a Mycenaean presence in the bay of Katapola, the island's history becomes less clear. During the 10th century BC Ionian settlers arrived, and the three cities of historic times emerged— *Aegiale, Minoa* and *Arkesine*: first, *Arkesine* colonised by Naxos, then *Minoa* by Samos, and *Aegiale* by Miletus. The mid-7th century BC poet, Semonides, was allegedly amongst the colonisers from Samos.

The island appears in the Athenian tribute lists from 433 BC paying one talent (compared with Kea's four talents, and

Paros's 18 talents). It participated in the Second Athenian
League in 357 BC. The fine Hellenistic towers and constructions on the island were put up during the uncertain times
when the island was first a possession of Macedonia, then
of the Ptolemies, and finally of the Rhodian State from the
end of the 3rd century BC. After 133 BC, the three cities were
assumed into the Roman Province of Asia. Amorgos was
often a place of exile in the Roman period, though clearly not one of the most punitive: Tacitus records that Ti-
berius commuted the proposed confinement of the hapless
Vibius Serenus on the barren island of Gyaros, into exile on
Amorgos, for humanitarian reasons (*Annals* IV, 29).

There is evidence of scattered Early Christian communities, especially in the bay of Katapola; but the increasing
frequency of pirate raids from the sea, pushed habitation
into the central uplands of the island, and the site of Chora
began to be enlarged and settled in the 9th century. The
arrival of refugee monks with the icon from Khoziba in
Palestine in this period, followed by the subsequent founding of the Chozoviótissa Monastery allegedly in 1088, was
of considerable importance for the history of the island.
Amorgos was taken by Geremia and Andrea Ghisi, on
behalf of the Duchy of Naxos of Marco Sanudo, in 1207.

As was common with the less central Cycladic islands, it subsequently changed hands many times; first ruled by the Ghisi family; regained between 1269 and 1296 by the Nicaean Emperor, John Vatatzes, and used principally as a place of exile; formally re-assigned to Venice by treaty in 1303 and governed by the Barozzi family; it was finally sold piecemeal in several stages to Giovanni Querini, Lord of Astypalaia, who possessed the island until its seizure by the Ottoman Admiral, Khaireddin Barbarossa in 1537. From 1540 it became formally a Turkish possession. A Turkish governor was installed at first, but by the 18th century the island was self-governing, paying tax to the Ottoman authorities for liberty of commerce and faith. The island was always a prey to piracy, culminating in one particularly fierce attack in 1797 by pirates from the Mani. In 1835 the island became part of the new Kingdom of Greece. In the same year a devastating fire spread from Aigiáli and burned the oak forests of Mount Kroukelos, radically altering the landscape and ecology of the northern end of the island.

The guide has been divided into three sections:
- *Central Amorgos*
- *Southwestern Amorgos*
- *Northeastern Amorgos*

CENTRAL AMORGOS: KATAPOLA, *MINOA*, CHORA & THE CHOZOVIOTISSA

(*For distances in text, Katapola port = 0.0km*)

Already from the approaching boat, the dramatic silhouette of the island anticipates the nature of its landscape. Like Ikaria or Hydra, Amorgós is a long mountainous breakwater in the sea. Looking over the empty waters to the south, the cliffs are often sheer and impenetrable. They are steep on the north side too, but relax sufficiently to afford two protected harbours in west-facing bays at Katápola and Aigiáli. These have historically been the principal approaches to the island. We begin at Katapola, in the centre of the north coast, which is the commonest point of disembarkation for ferries. The **bay of Katapola** cuts deep into the island: its springs and protected margins have supported Cycladic, Mycenaean, Greek, Roman, Early Christian and Mediaeval settlements, the remains of which are scattered around the shores of the bay. (*See plan p. 18.*)

THE BAY OF KATAPOLA

Katapola was developed during Roman times as the harbour for the ancient city of Minoa on the hill to the south: it was the lower city—'*kato polis*'—of the main settlement above. There are the remains of three **Roman tombs** of the 2nd century AD, at the western extremity of the waterfront, just beyond where the houses end. The largest had a layer of stucco in areas and was a small, private mausoleum of temple-like design. To its east, in the garden of the adjacent guest-house, are two small grave-loculi. Many pieces from Roman buildings and monuments are incorporated in the attractive church of the **Panaghia Katapolianí**, which lies 50m inland (south) of the small square on the waterfront. The church will have been rebuilt several times in its history; the present, 18th century structure is relatively plain inside, but its vaults are supported on ancient columns. The forecourt is a pleasing ensemble of many spolia: a votive inscription to 'Hermes of the auspicious road' (east end of church), a densely inscribed pedestal for an honorific statue, column fragments, and pieces of deeply carved Roman cornice reused as window sills and lintels in the south wall. Some of this material may come from a temple to Apollo *Pythios* which is attested in the area. The courtyard wall also in cludes pieces of Byzantine closure panels, indicating that there was an earlier church on this same site.

Following the waterfront track west beyond the Roman tombs, along the south side of the bay, you come to the small chapel of the **Panaghia** (0.5km), dedicated to the Nativity of the Virgin, and constructed almost entirely with blocks from a 4th or 5th century, Early Christian predecessor, which in turn had used pre-existing marble blocks from pagan buildings. The pieces are carved with a variety of designs—for example the delicately incised censor carved on the block to the north side of the door. In the interior (*key above door*), the altar is an eroded, but finely carved Composite capital in Naxian marble. The church, though old in origin, has clearly been rebuilt in the last 50 years. On the bluff above the church overlooking the bay, are traces of an Early Cycladic settlement. Further along the track is the late mediaeval, double church of the **Aghii Anargyri** (1km).

Almost contiguous with Katapola, inland from the east end of the bay, is the village of **Rachídi** (1km) built attractively along a low ridge. At the road junction on the shore below is the Katapola Community building in front of which several ancient fragments and pieces of Byzantine carving are displayed. The third community in the bay is **Xylokeratídi** (1.5km), the peaceful fishing village which looks onto the bay from the north shore and benefits from the excellent springs at 'Nerá' which rise in the valley a short distance to its west. A stepped path leads up and inland through the village: on the hillside to the west (*after passing the St George Varsamitis Hotel on your right*) is a **Mycenaean cemetery**. Most of the tombs, which date from the 13th and 12th centuries BC, have been disfigured with erosion but two remain, with the excavated chamber and a clear-cut *dromos* aligned a few degrees south of due east. On the hill beyond is the church of the **Evangelismós** (Annunciation), one of the oldest surviving churches on the island—dating from as early as the 9th century on the basis of vestiges of aniconic painting in its interior. (*Returning from the Mycenaean cemetery to the stone kalderimi, keeping always left, the path climbs the ridge between two gulleys. The church is hidden low in the western gulley. 20 mins by foot.*) The design is a dome on a square with a curious transverse barrel-vault tacked on to the east. The door in the south wall has been re-opened in recent times.

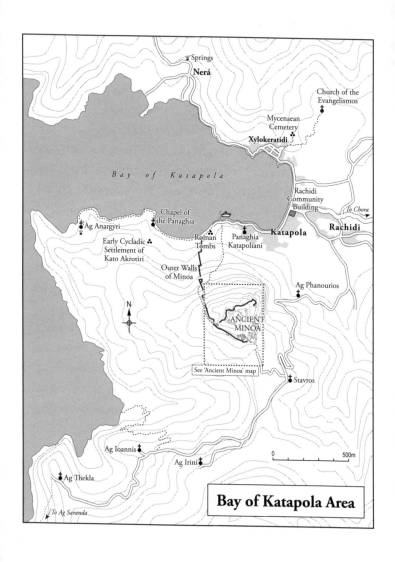

Springs
Nerá

Church of the
Evangelismos

Mycenaean
Cemetery

Xylokeratidi

B a y   o f   K a t a p o l a

Rachidi
Community
Building

To Chora

Chapel of
the Panaghia

Ag Anargyri

Roman
Tombs

Panaghia
Katapoliani

Katapola   **Rachidi**

Early Cycladic
Settlement of
Kato Akrotiri

Outer Walls
of Minoa

Ag Phanourios

N

ANCIENT
MINOA

See 'Ancient Minoa' map

Stavros

Ag Ioannis

0   500m

Ag Irini

Ag Thekla

To Ag Saranda

Bay of Katapola Area

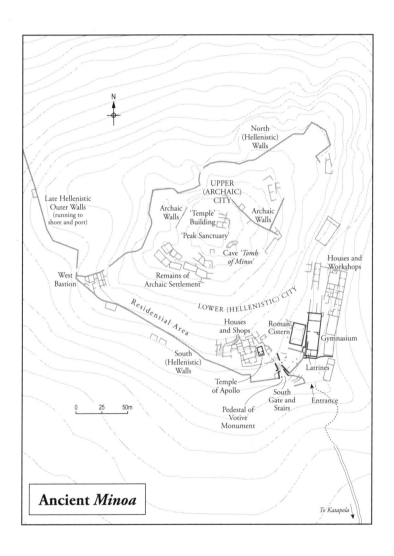

Ancient *Minoa*

ANCIENT *MINOA*

A path from the top of the habitation in Katapola leads up the hill of Minoa to the church of Aghios Phanourios and then on up the winding track to the archaeological site (*30 mins*): alternatively the motorable branch-road to the right, passing south of Rachidi, leads to the site in 3km. Of the three cities of antiquity on the island, the ruins of **Ancient Minoa* are the most extensive and interesting. It is an impressive site in an impressive position. (*Site always open and mostly unfenced.*)

History

The summit of the hill of Moundouliá, with its cave and rock formations, was inhabited in Late Neolithic times, as finds of obsidian and domestic artefacts of the period show. When the hill was subsequently settled in the 10th century BC, habitation moved to a more protected position on the south-facing slope of the hill: its remains have been indentified, along with the grand, Hellenistic buildings which are visible today. The settlement grew with the influx of colonisers from Samos and as a result the summit of the hill was fortified as an acropolis. Traces of the 8th century BC fortification-walls can be seen between rock outcrops on the north side of the summit and on the east slope. The city appears to have reached its apogee in the 4th century BC, when many of the buildings visible today were constructed. Under Roman domination greater importance was given to the port. The city had two poles—hill and harbour—connected by a single enceinte of walls. Latterly the harbour dominated, and the upper city was abandoned in the 4th century AD.

Name

Though it is clearly a possibility, the toponym '*Minoa*' (which is not unique in the Aegean) does not necessarily indicate a Cretan 'Minoan' connection. All we can say is that it probably refers to a legendary hero-founder, 'Minos': whether that was supposedly the Cretan Minos or another, we cannot know. Minoan peak sanctuaries at places where there are outcrops of rock are a common phenomenon in the Aegean: but there is as yet no archaeological evidence suggesting that there might have been one here of a clearly Minoan nature.

The site

There are two main areas: a lower site (mostly Hellenistic remains) on the south slope, and an upper site (with scattered Archaic and earlier remains) at the summit. On approaching the lower area, the well-constructed walls—some for fortification, some for retaining terraces, some for both—make an immediate impact. Viewed from the entrance, you see:

- **ahead and to the *right***, the terracing wall which supported the late 4th century BC **Gymnasium**, constructed in massive, interlocking masonry blocks with drafted edges, and channeled corners. On its left side, what looks like a postern gate at the head of a narrow channel, is in fact the drainage for the **latrines** which occupy the small wing made from massive stone blocks at the western end of the Gymnasium. The space still conserves its roof, and the **limestone benches cut with individual seats** over a drainage channel are unusually well-preserved inside. On the hillside directly above the Gymnasium rise large walls in a rough stone-rubble bound in mortar; these defined a **vaulted water cistern** of considerable size, which was constructed under Roman dominion in the 2nd century AD. The accumulated water must have supplied the gymnasium and its *thermae*, and provided drainage water for the latrines directly below. In later times, this vast ruined structure, which was always visible above ground, was referred to as 'Palatía'—an imagined 'palace' of Minos, the legendary founder, in the eyes of the local inhabitants of the area.

- **ahead and to the *left***, is the city's (main) **South Gate** in a trapezoid-shaped recess, with bastion-walls to either side; to the left of the approach is a votive pedestal; to the

right side, a **drainage channel** for rain-water, cut both
inside and outside the main threshold. The threshold
itself is a single block, shaped and cut to accommodate
the doors and their posts. Above the gate, slightly to the
left (west) is a small **temple to Apollo**, which faces south
from a platform of three marble steps. A fragment of
the lower portion of the **cult statue** has been set up in
the centre of the *naos:* its drill-cut, deeply folded dra-
pery dates it to around the late 3rd or 2nd century BC.
The temple would have been made entirely of the same,
hand-chiseled and finished marble-blocks which constitute its ruined base.

Both to left of the temple, and below and to the right of the
Gymnasium, a number **houses and shops** of the Hellenistic
town have been cleared by the archaeologists—many with
wells or cisterns for water still visible. Further around the
hill to the west, the remains of the houses have not been
cleared; but the line of the **enceinte of walls** is visible below them, becoming clearer as it approaches the **northwest
bastion**. Beyond the bastion, an arm of the walls, added in
Hellenistic times, continues steeply down the slope to the
port below.

Climbing up towards the summit from this point, the
scene changes: the geological conformation means that

there are natural rock terraces, plateaux, grottoes and outcrops, between which the base of stretches of the **Archaic
walls** (8th/7th century BC) can be seen. They come particularly into evidence on the east and southeast sides and are
quite different in construction from those below. The base
of a tower can be made out at the northeastern end.

The peak sanctuary is characterised by a rock summit
(255m a.s.l.), under which is a deep **natural cavern**, entered
by a small aperture—later fancifully dubbed the 'Tomb of
Minos'. The combination of the two—summit and cave—
constituted an obviously numinous site for prehistoric
man, and it is no surprise that Neolithic artefacts have been
found here going back to the 4th millennium BC. The cave
should not be thought of as separate from the cultic building or temple directly above it, whose outline can be seen
at the summit; together they formed the single unit of the
sanctuary. The finding of charcoal ash, sacrificial animal remains, horns and votive objects shows that cultic practices
occurred—but in honour of which divinity cannot yet be
determined. The sanctuary continued to be used into Hellenistic times and beyond, and objects relating to the cult of
Dionysos '*Minoites*' might suggest that, even in prehistoric
times before the appearance of Dionysos, the divinity was
also a god of the earth, and of fertility and procreation. It
is equally possible that the early cult was centred on a hero,

such as Minos, the legendary founder. The entrance to the sanctuary through the Archaic *peribolos*, or perimeter wall, has been rebuilt in Hellenistic times: similarly, the **sacred building or 'temple'** at the summit has been slightly adapted with time. But its form, like a small temple oriented east/west, with an inner sanctum or *naos*, and a forecourt to the east, follows the earliest construction which dates from the 8th century BC. The threshold can be seen, as well as ledges for the placing of offerings. Below the sanctuary area to the southwest, part of the **inhabited settlement of the Archaic period** has been uncovered.

The track leading to the southwest from the church of the Stavrós just below the archaeological site, continues into an area of considerable beauty. The two hamlets of untouched simplicity that you encounter, **Lefkés** and **Aghia Thekla** (*30 and 45 mins respectively by foot*) overlook attractive inlets with beaches. The churches in the area—Aghia Irini on the hillside above, **Aghios Ioannis** in Lefkes, and the **Aghii Saranda** (*60 mins*)—all incorporate ancient spolia. At Aghia Irini, an ancient sanctuary from Archaic through to Hellenistic times is attested.

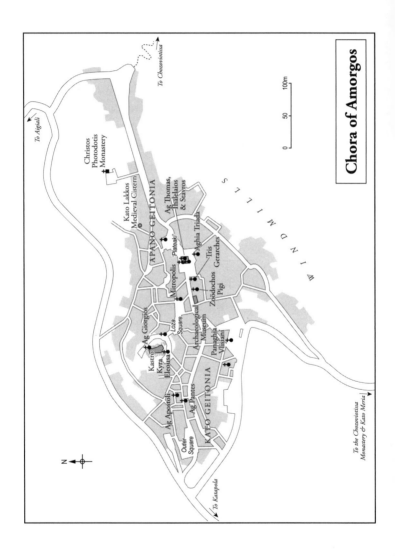

Chora of Amorgos

0   50   100m

To Agiali

To Chozoviotisa

Christos
Phorodotis
Monastery

Kato Lakkos
Medieval Cistern

APANO GEITONIA

Ag Thomas,
Thalelaios
& Stavros

Plateaki

Mitropolis

Aghia Triada

Tris
Gerarches

Zoödochos
Pigi

Ag Giorgios

Loza
Square

Archaeological
Museum

Kastro
Kyra
Eleousa

Panaghia
Vlisiani

Ag Apostoli

Ag Pantes

KATO GEITONIA

Outer
Square

WINDMILLS

N

To Katapola

To the Chozoviotisa
Monastery & Kato Meria

CHORA

Chora (5.2km) lies in a plateau at a height of 320m above sea level, invisible from the port and just below the watershed above the precipitous eastern side of the island. In the early morning and evening in the spring, clouds and mists often blow over the watershed strafing the buildings of the settlement. The town grew up during the 9th century AD, when insecurity from pirate attacks meant that the bay of Katapola was no longer viable for settlement and the population moved to this safer refuge. The original habitation clustered around the prong of rock which rises out of the plateau and formed the community's fortress: like the rock of Petra on Lesbos, this is the tip of a narrow volcanic 'plug'. It is crowned by the mediaeval **Kastro**, built in the 13th century by the Ghisi overlords. There is no space on the top of the rock-pinnacle for anything more than a tower (south end), a cistern, and a tight enceinte of walls. (*Access is by steep rock cut steps, through the church of Aghios Giorgios on the north side. Key for the gate is held either at the 'Loza' bar or at the 'Kallisti' patisserie in Chora.*) The Kastro must always have functioned as a look-out tower and refuge rather than as a residence. Immediately below on the south face, and partially overhung by the rock into which it is built, is the chapel of

the **Kyra [E]Leousa** ('Our Lady of Mercy'), which has the
appearance of a 10th or 11th century structure, but which
may occupy the site of an even earlier church which would
predate the development of the Chora.

The main body of Chora extends along two parallel,
winding thoroughfares between the open square at the
western entrance of the town in the 'Kato Geitoniá' (Lower Town) and the delightful *'Plateáki'* in the 'Apano Geitoniá' (Upper Town). *'Plateaki'* is surrounded by churches
and chapels and has several levels: at its centre, the undulating roofs of three contiguous chapels (St Thomas, St
Thalelaios and the Holy Cross, from north to south) seem
to grow from the ground. Fifty metres to the west of here
along the principal artery is a substantial 17th century
town-house with courtyard, known as the '**Gavras Man-
sion**' which houses the island's **Archaeology Museum**.
(*In high season, generally open daily 8.30–3, except Mon;
otherwise by appointment with the custodian, Giorgios
Vlavianós, T. 697 3396861.*) Many of the first items to be
found on Amorgos are now in the museum on Syros, and
many of the finest pieces are exhibited in Athens: material of interest, but of less importance, has been collected
here.

The attractive *downstairs courtyard* exhibits carved *stelai*, inscribed pedestals, a marble **standard for liquid-measures** for the market-place (*on shelf to right*), and fragments of Hellenistic and Roman sculpture. Of particular note is the reas-sembled clay, Archaic **burial urn**, complete with its lid and small decorative bands on the exterior; the skeleton and grave gifts are preserved inside.

The *upper level* contains cases with **pre-historic material**, decorated vases and bronze items from graves, including a fibia and a ring.

Of interest is the fragment of the shoulders and hair of an Archaic *kouros*, showing small traces of pigmentation; the colour appears to have been added substantially later than the date of the carving. There is a fine 5th century BC **grave-stele** with a full-standing figure relief, and several finely carved finials and *anthemia* from the roofs of Archaic and Classical buildings. Two cases contain grave finds from 4th century BC *Minoa*: terracotta figurines, relief-dec-orated bowls together with the moulds for their production, and items of **jewellery**—ear-rings and a pendant in gold.

An attractive feature of many of the buildings and churches in the same street and around the **Loza** ('Loggia') **Square** just to the north is that they incorporate ancient *anthemia* and marble *stelai* with carved funerary reliefs in their walls or gateways. A short distance northeast of the Plateaki, on the edge of an area of ruined houses to the right of the path, is the entrance into the **mediaeval cistern** of Chora, or 'Káto Lákkos', created probably at the time that the Kastro was built: it is a vaulted chamber, part excavated, part constructed, which still holds water to this day. Across the area of ruined buildings beyond stands the whitewashed complex of the **monastery of Christós Photodótis**, a dependency of the Chozoviótissa Monastery.

THE MONASTERY OF THE CHOZOVIOTISSA

A half-hour's walk by the road south of Chora, which rises to the watershed and then drops dramatically down the eastern side above the sea, brings you to one of the most extraordinary sights in the Aegean—the ***Monastery of the Panaghia Chozoviótissa** (7.7km), dedicated to the Presentation of the Virgin. (*Generally open daily 8.30–1, 4–sunset.*) The monastery hangs on an almost vertical cliff-face like an icon on a wall. Originally there would have been no whitewash to pick the monastery out from its improbable setting, and it would have receded almost invisibly into the rock-face from which it grew. The cliff at this point is almost 400m high, and the monastery is situated at about 260m above sea level.

The monastery structure

The buildings are in parts constructed, and in parts cut out from the rock-face. The botanist, Joseph Pitton de Tournefort, who visited in 1718, described the monastery as an '*armoire*'—a wardrobe or hanging cupboard—accurately describing how it consists of narrow shelves, one on top of another, closed by a façade, '*appliquée vers le bas d'un rocher effroyable*'. It is a model often used in Buddhist monasteries, less frequently with Orthodox monasteries. Its improbability as a structure and the imposing rock-face behind, evoke the world of the Desert Fathers, and it is perhaps no coincidence that the first monks who took refuge here were from the Syrian desert. Chozoviótissa has always been prone to damage from falling rocks; today it is strengthened by two massive buttresses on the front façade which have been added in the last century. In the summer of 1933, the Swiss-French architect, Le Corbusier visited Amorgos on a Mediterranean cruise: the flat white expanse of the monastery's façade, perforated with small windows, and the building's modular structure clearly left an impression on him whose influence can be seen in his work, especially the church of the Virgin at Ronchamp, begun in 1950.

Evolution of the Monastic community

Documentary evidence for the foundation is lacking; but a strong oral tradition maintains that the monastery received a charter from the Emperor in Byzantium, Alexios I Comnenus, in 1088—the same year in which the Monastery of St John on Patmos was founded. The tradition holds that the two were to be sister foundations with a formalised exchange of abbots, even though today the two monasteries are not bound by any special links. All the written documentation relating to Chozoviótissa dates from the 17th century or later; but all of it reinforces the oral tradition. The first monastic presence in small anchorites' caves on this cliff-face was probably during the 9th century when monks, fleeing from Arab incursions into Palestine, sought refuge here; such persecutions by Arab raiders are referred to by Theophanes. These monks probably brought with them their Holy Icon of the Virgin. If they and the holy icon were originally from the monastery in Khoziba, near Jericho, as tradition tells, this would explain the epithet '*Khozivítissa*' (as it should be), or 'Chozoviótissa' in modern usage. Between the 9th and the 11th century the community must have expanded rapidly, resulting in the Imperial chrysobull granting the monastery lands and rights, and initiating a building and renovation programme which brought into being the main monastery buildings. The structure underwent considerable restoration in the late 15th century, and has undergone small alterations since that time. The monastery was home in the 18th century to a hundred monks; the narrow terraces below the buildings were cultivated to produce beans, pulses, vegetables and pasture for goats, to sustain the community. Today there are three monks left.

Visiting the monastery

Entry is through a low narrow doorway with a marble frame, artlessly decorated with fig and vine motifs. Above it is a blind arch in *poros* stone, surrounded on the outside with decorative *phialostomia*; its pointed form—of clearly western influence—also suggests that this outer doorway was constructed during the period of Venetian occupation, perhaps as late as the 1480s. Immediately inside is a water-stoup set in a painted niche; opposite it, the fine 19th century strong-box of the monastery now contains spare clothing for visitors. Steps lead up through the rock to the upper level of the sacristy and to the narrow vaulted space of the *catholicon* which hugs the precipice—the living rock forming its north side and a wall, its south side. The original **icon of the *Virgin of Khoziba*** is on the south wall, so darkened and covered with silver revetment that nothing can be said of its age other than it is believed to date from the early 9th century—the period immediately after the iconoclastic debate.

The icons which currently adorn the iconostasis are all of the
17th century or later, but of particularly high quality none-
theless; the same is true of those, such as the beautiful *Christ
in Majesty*, displayed along the north wall of the *catholicon*.

The **Sacristy** at Chozoviótissa is of particular interest for
its important collection of Byzantine manuscripts. Much of
the monastery's library has perished, but the twenty-three
Byzantine codices on parchment still in its possession date
from the 10th to the 19th centuries. Only a few are exhibited at any one time: two items customarily on show are the
exquisitely illuminated **Evangelistaries** of the 11th and 13th
centuries respectively. Some of the monastery's plate and a
section of fine liturgical **embroideries** of the 18th century
are also on show.

To acquire a keener sense of the landscape which the
founding monks of Chozoviótissa inhabited, a foot-path
east from the monastery can be taken, leading to two of its
hermitic dependencies on the southern slope of Mount
Prophitis Elias which rises 700m from the sea below. The
path lies across an impressive landscape whose gradients
are not for the faint-hearted. The ruined hermitage church
of **Aghios Ioannis Chrysóstomos** (c. 290m a.s.l.) which
conserves areas of damaged, 18th century wall-painting is
reached in 35 minutes' walk by the lower branch from the

junction you encounter after 20 minutes; and the rock-hewn chapel of **Panaghia Theoskepastí** (c. 450m a.s.l.) in 55 minutes by the upper branch. The *walk can be followed beyond along the ridge of the island, passing via Asfondilítis after 2 hours, and finally descending through Apáno Potamós to Aigiáli in c. 4 hours.

SOUTHWESTERN AMORGOS

AGHIOS GIORGIOS VARSAMITIS, STAVROS, MARKIANI AND KAMARI

From Chora the road to the south of the island closely follows the watershed of the island with magnificent views alternating to either side. After 4km the monastery of **Aghios Giorgios Varsamítis**, or Balsamitis, (9.5km) is indicated to the right. The monastery sits at the head of a valley rich with springs of water and is surrounded by a small oasis of cultivation: the church itself is built over a weak spring, while above and to its west, the rising water was sufficient to drive a water-mill which still survives. The present 17th century structure, built over earlier churches on this same site, is a dependency of the

Chozoviótissa. It acquired fame through its 'water oracle' which centred on a marble basin or urn which filled and emptied with water miraculously, responding to queries and giving auspices by its actions. This curious phenomenon was observed and recorded in some detail by Pitton de Tournefort when he visited the church in 1718. The oracle may be a successor to a pagan oracle on the site. At the south end of the narthex is an *aghiasma* or sacred rock-pool of spring water; this is not the 'oracle', however, which was separate and kept at some distance from it. Small areas of the interior are covered with 17th and 18th century **wall-paintings**—images of *St John the Baptist* and the *Virgin and Child* on the north pillar of the vault. A curiosity of the church is a number of **graffiti** of fish in the pavement around the north door.

Further west, the main road climbs again onto a saddle, on the western edge of which sits the complex of churches of the **Stavrós** (12.5km)—a series of four contiguous, barrel-vaulted units, two with apses, one with a belfry. The interior makes the arrangement clearer—namely a symmetrical 12th century church with two side-aisles separated by arches supported on pieces of antique architrave, and a separate, parallel chapel dedicated to St Nikitas which was added later to the south and has the remains of an image of the Baptist next to the apse. The paving of the main church would appear to be that of a pagan or Early Christian structure, and the altar comprises a closure slab from an early *templon*, suggesting that the complex occupies the site of a much earlier place of worship. The area marked the boundary between the territories of *Arkesine* and *Minoa*, and a rock bearing the incised word '*OPOΣ*', 'boundary', has been found in the fields beyond the sharp west turn in the road, 300m after Stavrós.

The most significant Early Cycladic site explored so far on Amorgos, known as **Markianí**, occupies the rock outcrop and summit just to the left (south) of the road at 14.5km. To the north and south sides of the outcrop the foundation walls of dwellings are visible, and the outline of a fortification wall around can be traced in stretches: this 'acropolis' enceinte possessed semicircular bastions. The bold site, which sits on the summit looking out over the water to Astypalaia, Anaphi and Santorini, may have been inhabited for as long as eight centuries, beginning around 2800 BC. Excavations since 1985 on the southern slope have brought to light artefacts of a predominantly practical, domestic and commercial nature, including a wide variety of tools, and some lead and clay seals. The latter point to a high degree of organised commercial exchange.

The practical finds from Markianí contrast notice-
ably with the ritual objects, such as the marble figurines,
generally retrieved from cemeteries. One very important
source of these has been the cemeteries excavated in the
area of **Dokathismata**, which lies not far from Markianí
(*2km as the crow flies to the north of the conical hill of Poú-
los visible to the northwest*). The style of figurines from
the excavations here is quite distinct, with a much greater
emphasis on line than volume. The 'Dokathismata type'
is predominantly flatter in profile, with much wider, slop-
ing shoulders, tapering to thin calves and ankles, giving
an overall pentagonal form to the thorax and abdomen.
They bear careful incisions which define the forms. Although it may not appear so at first sight, there is considerable stylistic variety within the corpus of Cycladic
figurines.

At 16.5km the road descends to the settlement of
Kamari; beside the final bend in the road before the village is the church of **Aghios Nikolaos** whose contiguous,
undulating vaults present an appearance similar to that
of the Stavrós. Once again it is a triple-aisled church, with
an attached *parecclesion* to the north, built probably in
the 14th or 15th century over the site of an ancient predecessor. The interior is decorated with **wall-paintings**
which are currently being restored.

ANCIENT *ARKESINE*

The northward branch of the asphalt road from Kamari ends after 1km at the village of **Vroútsi** (17.5km), from where it is a steep, 30-minute descent by foot to the site of **Ancient *Arkesine***. On the descent, the path passes below the large, modern church of **Aghios Ioannis Apokephalistís** ('St John the Beheaded'); it is dramatically sited on a prominent bluff on the hillside which is believed to have been occupied in antiquity by a sanctuary of Athena *Itonia* (an unusual epithet for the goddess, associating her cult here with that in the city of Iton in Phthiotis).

Arkesine, founded by settlers from Naxos in the 8th century BC occupies an exposed and panoramic promontory of the north coast: Donousa lies directly ahead; Naxos, Keros and Herakleia to the west; and the long extent of the rest of the island, to the east. The natural site provides a promontory, capped with a limestone outcrop ideal for fortification as an acropolis; but it offers little that could have functioned as a protected harbour nearby. The city's main out-port must have been at some distance—perhaps even as far as Kato Kambos Bay to the west. As you descend the path, the best preserved stretch of **fortification wall** can be seen below and to the right of the acropolis rock, in large isodomic masonry with later walling built on top. Further well-conserved elements of the **bastions** and fortifications lie further round the steep, eastern side of the promontory and are best seen from the summit above. In spite of the city's importance in Antiquity, little remains visible other than fortifications and gates. The acropolis today is occupied by the remains of a fortified, mediaeval *kastro*: the cisterns and millstones lying around are mediaeval; most of the potsherd-scatter is mediaeval, too; but some of the constructions, such as that opposite the front of the church of the Panaghia Kastrianí, incorporate ancient blocks bearing inscriptions. The site awaits proper excavation.

ANCIENT TOWER AT AGHIA TRIADA

Much of the wealth of Arkesine depended on its protected and cultivable hinterland—especially the alluvial **Káto Meriá plateau**, now occupied by the modern settlement called **Arkesíni** (19.5km), and formerly referred to as 'Chorió'. Such an area, with its relatively good soil and hidden location, was of great value in the Cycladic Islands. Evidence that its cultivation and produce needed adequate protection is provided by the conspicuous presence in the middle of the area of a large tower with an attached complex of fortified, farm-buildings. The ***Hellenistic tower at Aghia Triada** (20.2km), 700m north of Arkesíni, is impressively large and well-preserved and is one of the most signal monuments of its type in the Aegean. It dates probably from the late 4th century BC— the same period as the (circular) tower and complex of Heimaros in southern Naxos, to which it bears some similiarities.

The complex has overall a T-shaped plan—a large, multifunctional rectangular block (25.3 x 11.4m) in front, with a strongly fortified tower (7m x 7m) protruding from the centre of one of the long sides. The whole construction is a monument to the precision and eloquence of **Hellenistic masonry**. On the front façade, the massive blocks of the lowest courses merge into more regular, parallel, interleaved courses of isodomic masonry above, rising to a height of 5.6m in the tower. The corners, as always, are perfectly drafted. The design of the masonry varies intriguingly: the west wall of the tower, for example incorporates large trapezoidal blocks which alter the effect of its overall design. The walls are of double thickness, lined with an inner shell in smaller stone blocks. The front rectangular area is articulated into several divisions and must have had two floors, as the steps on the south side indicate. A number of the **threshold-blocks** are single monoliths measuring up to 2.8m in breadth: most bear the swing-post holes for what were clearly very substantial doors. Security was foremost in every consideration.

The **tower block** is once again constructed with double-walls, and is entered by a door whose frame and **lintel-block** cannot fail to impress. In the lateral jambs the bolt-bar holes indicate the size of the transom which secured the door. The lower level of the tower is filled solid, except for a square space immediately in front of the door. This would have accommodated steps leading up to the main level; but it also created a defensive feature, in that any intruder would be caught vulnerably in the bottom of a stair-well on entering. The tiny apertures on the upper level are shaped as embrasures—an early example of the use of the feature. In the corner is a small niche: not a chimney—perhaps a small aedicule for an image.

Impressive as these towers are as pieces of human ingenuity, we know little about how they functioned. This tower had no use as a look-out or advance defence post, because it is constructed in a declivity encircled by hills. There are no mines or quarries for minerals in the vicinity here, which might have justified such doughty walls for secure storage of valuable materials. Affording protection to valuable agricultural produce is one explanation put forward for such buildings; yet the fertility of this area is hardly such as to merit the considerable human effort involved in raising such a massive building. The tower will most probably have functioned as a fortress or place of refuge for the entire rural community that worked the fields in the area. They were some distance away from the safety of their city (*Arkesine*) and were closer to the shores and inlets by which danger could arrive. A tower such as this was a 'local acropolis' for them. Its size and strength tell us two things: the rural community was quite large, and the expected danger was great.

Due south from the tower at Aghia Triada rises **Mount Kórax** (524 m). On its eastern shoulder, at '**Pyrgí**', was another rectangular tower of the Hellenistic period, whose base is visible, incorporated into a later farm-building. This must have communicated with the larger tower in the valley and functioned as its look-out post. On the discrete rise further to the east, at Kástelas, an Early Cycladic acropolis has been identified.

THE WESTERN EXTREMITY OF THE ISLAND

From Arkesíni the road continues west and descends to **Kolophána** (22km): to the right, below the road (400m before Kolophána) are some ruined buildings with a small, white, flat-roofed structure in their midst. This is the remarkable church of the *Panaghia tou Polití (also known locally as the 'Panaghia Giorgianí'): once a small temple in the midst of a protected and fertile area, it is now a chapel with three ancient columns and capitals (2 Doric, 1 Ionic) supporting a roof of ancient stone rafters. All around the immediate area lie other fragments of column bases, capitals, altars and part of an antique, stone olive-press.

The continuation of the road west from Kolophána finishes at the delightful **bay of Paradísa** (23km), looking out to the offshore islet of Krambousa. The bay takes its name from the '*parádeisos*' (the enclosed area in front of a church) belonging to an **Early Christian chapel**, whose remains can be seen about 15m back from the shore on the north side of the cove. The outline of the small church and its enclosure, its north wall, apse, and some of the paved floor, are all still visible. This harbour would have provided the shortest and most protected crossing to Naxos, via Keros.

The track which branches north from Kolophána leads a further 2.5km to **Káto Kámbos Bay**—the only truly protected inlet at this end of the island. It is a well-hidden haven at the head of a protected creek, with fertile fields directly behind the shore. The secluded coastal site is typical of those favoured by Early Christian communities for their churches, and it is no surprise to find that the chapel of **Aghios Ioannis Theologos** at the eastern side of the inlet is built into what remains of the east end of an **Early Christian basilica**. There are steps cut into the rock and many ancient spolia, including straight-fluted and twist-fluted columns, both inside the chapel and in the immediate area. A fine early Christian capital has been set on end in the stone wall to the south of the chapel. Even the small, 1950s church of the Dormition of the Virgin, on the water front to the west, includes a section of frieze with triglyphs in its front wall. The bay is often the haunt of Lesser egrets; and in the wider area of the valley between here and Aghia Triada there are Sardinian warblers; while at the eastern end of the island, the rarer Rüppell's warbler is an occasional visitor.

NORTHEASTERN AMORGOS

FROM CHORA TO AIGIALI

Until the construction of the road northeast from Chora along the mountain ridge to Aigiáli in the mid-1980s, the two parts of the island functioned as separate entities, linked only by caïques and occasional ferries. For this reason the island still has two ports with separate ferry schedules.

After passing a junction (11km), from which a branch track (right) rounds the summit of the mountain and doubles back to the cave hermitage of the Panaghia Theoskepastí (*see p. 35*) above Chozoviótissa, the road descends with good views of the off-shore island of Nikouriá. Before a sharp right bend, the church of Aghios Ioannis Prodromos (13km) at **Ríchti** is clearly visible below the road to the left; above it stand the ruins of a **Hellenistic tower**, almost 9m in diameter. The doorway was in the south side, where the wall still stands to a considerable height, constructed in parallel courses of massive, interlocking blocks of different dimensions. This is one of a chain of such towers which survey the sea-routes along the north coast and which survive in various degrees of ruination: there are a further five along the north slope between here and Katapola, and three between here and Aigiáli (including the one to the south of Asfonidilítis on the opposite, south-facing slope). Sixteen Hellenistic towers have been located on Amorgos so far.

At 15km the branch-road (right) leads up the narrow gorge to the saddle between the north and south slopes of the island and ends at the semi-abandoned settlement of **Asfondilítis**, overlooking the sea in solitary isolation. No new building or paved street disturbs a scene which could almost have stepped from the Bronze Age—stone huts and byres on a rocky plateau where little other than the prickly-pear now grows. Only two whitewashed dwellings and the compact, double-aisle church of **Aghios Nikolaos** attest any human presence. The village lies on the main pathway from Chozoviótissa to Aigiáli. The wider area, known as Kápsala, supported an Early Cycladic settlement whose cemeteries have provided notable marble figurines and sculptures.

After the Asfondilítis junction, the road descends rapidly to the north coast at the point where the long eastern arm of the **islet of Nikouriá** almost touches the shore. Were it not for the 200m wide channel of 'Kakopérato' that separates the two land masses, Nikouriá would have been a headland, defining a third, west-facing bay similar

to those of Katapola and Aigiáli. The chapel of the Panaghia on Nikouriá, opposite the harbour of Aghios Pavlos
(15km), is a mediaeval foundation; otherwise the islet is
uninhabited. The straits were surveyed once again by a
Hellenistic tower whose remains are visible on the hillside
600m due south of the narrows. From here the road follows the shore to Aigiáli.

AIGIALI, LANGADA, THOLARIA & THE
EASTERN END OF THE ISLAND

The attractive harbour town of **Aigiáli** (20km), often ab-
breviated to 'Yiáli', occupies a privileged position in an
ample and protected bay, ringed with majestic mountains.
A fertile alluvial '*kambos*' extends inland of the shore. The
limestone mountains, particularly to the south, spring
fresh water: they were once mantled in oak forests. The
geographical configuration has some similarities to the
bay of Katapola, but is grander and more beautiful. The
coast and harbour show signs mainly of a Roman presence: marble fragments scattered in the village; the pedestal of a votive statue in the small *plateia* to the east; and
the remains of walls in Roman constructional materials
a short distance before the north end of the long, sandy
beach of the town.

Ancient *Aegiale* lay high above this area to the north, near the village of **Tholaria** (22.5km). (*Take first street uphill from just below the outer plateia of Tholaria, then immediately left; path leads off right towards hill top. 15 mins.*) Once again the position of the site is striking. To the northwest, the land falls away into the fjord of Mikrí Vlicháda and to the sea 200m below. To the northeast, the protective height of Mount Koutelós rises 433m from the shore. Magnificent **views** extend in all directions. The site has not been excavated, but evidence of the city lies on the surface, in particular at the rocky summit of the ridge where the bedrock has been cut and shaped at several points. Much of the fallen masonry of houses has been reused in the terracing of the slopes by farmers, but at several points on the north and east both the line and material of the **fortification-walls** are clear. The northern tip of Amorgos constitutes an important landfall in open waters and a commercial node between the Cyclades and the Dodecanese and Asia Minor. *Aegiale*, as a Milesian foundation of the 8th or 7th century BC, was well placed to profit from this. A site more different from the fertile river estuary of the mother-town of Miletus, though, cannot be imagined.

The ancient city's presence extended over the wider area. Traces of further defensive walls have been found

at Tholária, where the church of the **Aghii Anargyri** rises
on what is thought to be the site of an ancient temple,
and the entrance-gate to the church itself comprises an
assemblage of antique fragments. By the church of the
Taxiarch at **Astratios** (*35 mins walk due east of Tholaria*)
are the remains of a rectangular tower and farmstead of
the Hellenistic period. Further southeast again (*more easily reached by the good path from Langáda—see below*), at
the church of the **Panaghia Epanochorianí**, was the site
of another sanctuary, possibly dedicated to Athena; little
remains to be seen but for the central marble *anthemion*
of an ancient temple which is immured into the façade
of the modern church. Slightly to the south stands the
earlier, domed 15th century church of **Aghios Ioannis
Pródromos**.

Tholariá itself is a village of great charm and tranquil-
lity, with stacked streets, covered walkways, and wide
views both to west and to north. The surrounding natural landscape on the north side of the amphitheatre of
Aigiáli Bay differs substantially from that of Langáda
(24km) on the south side. The south side is hard limestone, rich in water and vegetation; the north side is a
gravelly, arenaceous rock, giving rise to the eroded contours of a more typically 'Cycladic landscape'. The combination of the two, the grandeur of the mountains that

surround the wide, west-facing bowl, and the bay itself which embraces the pleasing form of the island of Nik-ouriá, constitute one of the loveliest *landscapes in the Cyclades. It is seen to perfection as the sun declines in the early evening. The steep mountain slopes on the south side of the bay, with their frequent springs, have given rise to several villages of well-preserved architectural unity: **Apáno** and **Káto Potamós** to the west and **Langáda** to the east, overlooking the area from high up on a slope of rocks, cactus and small oak. All these villages grew up in the early Middle Ages as part of the general retreat to safety away from the shores and the piracy that infested the coasts. The rock church of **Aghia Triada**, which sits on a ledge in the cliff to the south of the road just before arriving in Langáda, may have first been used as a hiding place during attack from pirates. The rock pinnacles in the gorge below Langáda to the north, also provided a different kind of refuge; the inaccessible and half-deserted *borgo* of **Stroumbos** must first have been built as such. The gorge around it provides a micro-climate in which varieties of acacia, arbutus, broom and olive crowd the rocks and the elusive Rüppell's warbler may be seen. The area is of great beauty.

From the northeastern extremity of Langáda, a foot-path leads up towards the eastern end of the island. After 15 minutes the paved path continues round to the left to the Panaghia Epanochorianí, referred to above; the stepped path to the right climbs steeply for another hour before reaching the *monastery of Aghios Ioannis Theologos. The way is through dense *maquis*, and in the occasional breaks of oaks that shade the path nightingales can be heard in spring. The monastery is believed to have been established as early as the 9th century, though what stands today dates from 500 years later, at the time it became a dependency of the Chozoviótissa. It dominates a small, fertile plateau, which provided its living, in the saddle between the peaks of Mount Kroúkelos to the south and Mount Skopós immediately to the northwest. The monastery and its surrounding buildings are empty now.

The *catholicon* is heavily buttressed on the south side, and the dome and roof have been rebuilt in recent restoration. The interior (*key under stone by door*) is unexpectedly spacious with three aisles and a wide apse, furnished with a **synthronon** and a central abbot's seat. In the conch are fragments of **wall-painting** of considerable quality: the fine and highly stylised facial features remaining, suggest a date in the late 13th or 14th century. The altars in all three apses are composed of **ancient capitals and fragments**, confirming what has been inferred from other remains in the area that this was probably a small sanctuary in Antiquity, with possible continuity into early Christian times. Noteworthy is the **protrusion of natural rock** in the north side of the interior—a symbolic memory of the Rock of the Cave of St John the Divine on Patmos, to whom this church is dedicated.

Not far beyond the monastery, the land drops precipitously to the sea over 300m below. The whole northern coast and eastern promontory of the island is an unrelenting wall of cliffs which, directly to the south of here, reach their culmination below the peak of the island, **Mount Kroúkelos** (823m). Out to sea to the east can normally be seen the islets of *Kinaros* and *Lebinthos* (modern Levitha) which though waterless and uninhabited were important landmarks and stepping stones for mariners making the crossing of the open waters from the Cyclades to Kos, Kalymnos and Asia Minor. A path, which crosses the plateau and rises up the slope of Kroukelos opposite the monastery, leads to the remote church of the **Stavros** (75–90 minutes beyond) on a rock-saddle below the peak of Pramatevtís (720m), commanding immense views both to north and south. In the gorge to the south side were the island's Bauxite mines, which operated at the beginning of the last century. The mountain's greatest resource was once its forest of oaks which covered the

north-facing slopes of Kroukelos, and were nourished by
the frequent vernal and autumnal mists which strafe the
summit moistening the northern slopes. The forests dis-
appeared in a conflagration which burned for three weeks
in 1835.

Returning to the bay once again, the sensation of descending into the cavea of a large theatre towards a stage
of sea with the islet of Nikouriá as the backdrop, is yet
more vivid for having seen the ring of mountain cliffs
which enclose the northern end of the island.

PRACTICAL INFORMATION

840 08 **Amorgós**: area 121sq km; perimeter 126km; resident population 1,851; max. altitude 823m. **Port Authority**: T. 22850 71259. **Information**: Synodinos Travel (Katápola), T. 22850 71747 or 71201, www. amorgos.net

ACCESS

Amorgos lies at the terminus of a ferry-route; it is a minimum 7–8 hr journey (often longer) between Piraeus and the island, with several stops en route—always including either Naxos or Paros. *Blue Star Ferries* operates the service daily in the summer and five days a week in winter, alternating between the island's two ports: Katápola, the principal destination, in the centre, and Aigiáli ('Egiáli', 'Yáli') 20km further north. It is important for any itinerary to establish which of the two is the port of arrival/departure. *Blue Star* also connects Aigiáli (only) with Astypalaia three times weekly. The *F/B Express Skopelitis*, based in Katápola, plies through the Lesser Cyclades to Naxos and returns daily in summer, always stopping at Koufonisi, Schoinousa and Herakleia en route, also including Aigiáli and Donousa three times weekly. The service runs from April–end Oct, weather permitting. The *Blue Star* services maintain connections with these smaller islands 2–3 times a week in winter.

LODGING

Two small, comfortable hotels provide welcoming and attractive solutions in the medium price-range: the **'Emprostiada' Traditional Guest House** (in a new building, but of traditional design) in the heart of Chora (*T. 22850 71013, fax 71814, www. amorgos-studios.amorgos.net*); and the more conventional **Hotel Vigla** (*T. 22850 73288, fax 73332, www.vigla-hotel. amorgos.net*) in the hill-town of Tholaria, above Aigiáli. Offering simpler facilities, are: the **Pension Amorgos**

on the harbour-front of Katapola (same management and numbers as Emprostiada above); in the village of Langáda, **Artemis Rooms** (*T. 22850 73226, www.amorgos-studios.amorgos.net; open all year*); the same owners also rent rooms on the beach near Aigiáli. Highly recommended for visits to Amorgos based around walking, riding, historic sightseeing, botanising and bird-watching, are *Spe**cial Interest Holidays** who offer an excellent range of civilised activities and places to stay (*T. 693 982 0828, www. special-interest-holidays.com*).

EATING

Some of the best food is to be found in the island's small rural villages: the taverna **Gior-**

galinis in Vroútsi and **Marouso** in Arkesíni (Chorió), in the west; or **Sandouraki** in Tholaria at the north end of the island. **Katina's To Limani** at Aigiáli serves some of the best seasonal and traditional Greek fare on the island, and is popular with local families, especially on Sundays. More rarified, but offering some interesting *mezes,* is **To Chima** in the heart of Chora.

FURTHER READING

Lila Marangou, *The Monastery of the Panaghia Khozoviotissa*, Athens 2005. The author is indebted to the writings of Prof. Lila Marangou on archaeological matters which constitute the most complete and authoritative account of the island's monuments.

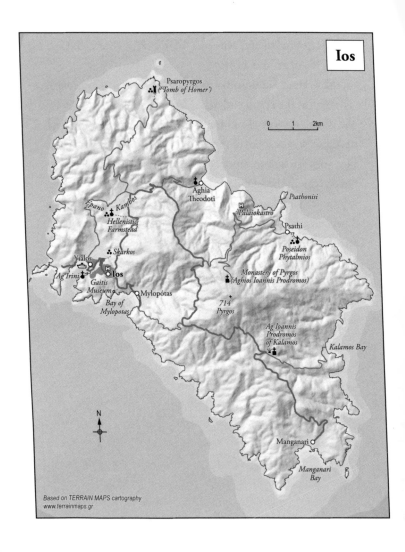

Ios

Psaropyrgos
('Tomb of Homer')

Aghia
Theodoti

Psathonisi

Palaiokastro

Psathi

Épano   Kambos

Hellenistic
Farmstead

Poseidon
Phytalmios

Skarkos

Monastery of Pyrgos
(Aghios Ioannis Prodromos)

Yialos

Ag Irini

Ios

Gaitis
Museum

Mylopótas

714
Pyrgos

Bay of
Mylopotas

Ag Ioannis
Prodromos
of Kalamos

Kalamos Bay

N

Manganari

Manganari
Bay

0   1   2km

Based on TERRAIN MAPS cartography
www.terrainmaps.gr

IOS

For its size, Ios was once one of the least populated of the Cycladic islands. The scale and wildness of its mountainous interior beyond the two fertile valleys behind the main city, hindered its development. The construction of roads and a boom in tourism in recent years have altered that, inevitably compromising to some degree the island's solitary beauty and grandeur. Ios has a picturesque Cycladic *chora* and a number of the finest beaches in the Aegean; these have attracted a very visible and sometimes dissonant kind of tourism to the island whose impact, concentrated in Chora and around the two beautiful bays of Ormos and Milopotas on the west coast, has ballooned in the last decade. Outside this area, however, the island has retained much of its former character: the rural, fertile valley of Epano Kambos, where the existence of the remains of a Hellenistic farm-building indicate the area's agricultural significance to the ancient city; the deserted north of the island, where Homer—according to tradition—was supposed to have been shipwrecked and buried; the deep, eastern bays overlooked by the remnants of a castle high on the promontory of Palaiokastro; and the volcanic, boulder-strewn landscape of the south, which ends in the magnificent sweep of Manganari Bay looking south to Santorini. New roads have also made more accessible two of the remotest monasteries of the Cyclades: the ancient and superbly panoramic monastery of Aghios Ioannis Prodromos, just below the island's 713m peak, and Aghios Giorgios of Kalamos, buried in a landscape reminiscent of that of the hermitages of the Desert Fathers in Egypt. At every turn, Ios surprises with the variety of its landscape.

In Antiquity there were important settlements on Ios: the first was a flourishing and sophisticated prehistoric urban centre at Skarkos, just behind Ormos Bay, dating from the 3rd millennium BC, where ongoing excavations are uncovering the walls of two-storey buildings, well-planned streets and squares; the second, Ancient *Ios*, was on the strategic site of the modern town. It must have been a large city, given the size and circumference of its remaining fortification walls. The finds from both these sites are collected together in a new museum on the ground floor of the island's Town Hall.

Modern Ios provides important lessons in the sociological and environmental impact of tourism on a small Mediterranean island. A vulnerable but stable local economy, based on agricultural production (fruit and cotton) and a variety of small family enterprises which had sustained the island throughout recent centuries, has been swept away almost overnight by the demands made by tourism for buildings, modes of transportation, employees and imported goods which have little or nothing to do with Ios, its traditions and its landscape. Recent changes in the local administration suggest that there is a will to redress some of the worst imbalances; but the damage to the island's traditional social structure is already done. None of this, however, is a reason for not visiting what is still a beautiful and interesting island. Ios can be unexpectedly delightful in the quieter months.

HISTORY

The inlet of Ormos and its fertile hinterland were settled in the 3rd millennium BC: the sophistication of the settlement and the quality of the finds at Skarkos have recently brought Ios to the forefront of prehistoric archaeology. Smaller settlements of the same period have been identified at other coastal sites: at Manganari, Plakes, Aghia Theodoti, Plakotos, and on the islet of Psathonisi. Ios had Phoenician and Mycenaean contacts from before the 12th century BC, and Ionians settled in the 10th century; but the island has so far yielded virtually no remains of significance from the Geometric period.

According to a strong tradition, Homer, whose mother, Clymene, may have hailed from Ios, was shipwrecked, died and buried on the island. According to Pausanias visitors in Antiquity were shown his grave, and its presence on the island is referred to by both Pliny and Strabo—although none of these writers had been to Ios and seen it. By the 6th century BC, Ios was a small city-state. Like its Ionian-settled neighbours to the north, it was early on a member of the Athenian league; was under Macedonian rule from 338 BC; and after 220 BC was allied with Rhodes. Remnants of Roman infrastructure suggest that Ios was not merely a place of exile under Roman rule, but also an active trading centre.

With the demise of Roman power, the sheltered and hidden inlet of Ormos became a base for piracy, and the population moved into the fortified sites of the interior. Ios was one of the original islands constituting the Duchy of Naxos of Marco Sanudo in the aftermath of the Fourth Crusade. It was briefly recaptured for Byzantium by the renegade admiral, Licario, in 1278/9, but was again under Venetian control by 1296 in the form of the Schiavi family who held the island as a fief of the Duchy of Naxos, until by marriage it passed first to the Crispo family at the end of the 14th century, and then to the Pisani family, who held onto it until Khaireddin Barbarossa captured Ios for the Ottoman Sultan in 1537. In the first Russo-Turkish War of 1770–74, Ios was occupied by Russian forces along with the other Cyclades. Ios contributed 24 ships and crews to the cause of the Greek War of Independence in 1821 and was united with the liberated Greek State in 1829. The island was much visited by the poet, Odysseas Elytis, and was latterly home to the painter, Yiannis Gaitis (1923–84), in whose memory a small museum of modern art is currently being created between Chora and Milopotas.

ORMOS BAY & SKARKOS HILL

(Chora = 0.0km for distances in text)

Ios had no mineral, and only meagre agricultural, wealth: its two assets in earlier times were its plentiful timber and its sheltered and deeply indented port of **Ormos Bay** (2km). Later, however, the harbour became a liability for the island when it was adopted by pirates as a safe and invisible refuge. It is still today one of the most attractive and protected inlets in the Cyclades, lined with beaches and framed by hills which partially hide the island's *chora* from view. On the east side of the inlet, visible from the arriving ferry, is the 17th century church of **Aghia Irini**, one of the island's grandest buildings, with two striking domes and belfries. The oldest church in the area, **Aghios Giorgios**, lies in a small open area about 250m inland of the harbour to the right of the road to Chora, sunk down into the ground which with time has risen all around it. The pillars of a former narthex or loggia in front of the west door still stand, but the roof they supported is gone. The church itself is a beautiful piece of 13th or 14th century architecture, with a generous dome which covers the entire area of its square floor-plan. From the bend in the road just beyond the church, the old, stepped *kalderimi* leads from the port—which today is called simply **Yialos**, or 'shore'—up to Chora. The partly shaded climb only takes 15 minutes and is the most enjoyable way of reaching the old town from the port.

One of the most interesting prehistoric sites in the Cyclades lies a little over a kilometre inland of the main beach of Ormos, grouped around the low discrete hill called *Skarkos (2.5km), to the northeast side of the valley behind. The site is of particular interest for the remarkable state of preservation of its meticulously constructed buildings and streets, as well as for the copious finds which have come to light during excavations. (*No official opening times as yet, as excavations continue. The site is reached by taking either one of the two rough-stone tracks which head north from opposite the filling station behind Yialos.*)

The densely-built settlement being uncovered on the north-west side of the hill dates from the mid-3rd millennium BC (Early Cycladic II period) and covers an area in excess of a hectare. The sea probably reached as far as the foot of the hill at the time it was first settled, leaving fertile land for cultivation to the north and west of the site. The notable quality of construction of the houses is clear even to the non-specialist eye. The carefully built stone walls stand 2–3m high, and bear remarkable refinements: in places there is a 'string-course' of protruding schists, which may have served to separate plastered from un-rendered areas of the wall; the threshold blocks have been carefully selected and set; and at some points the thickness of the wall accommodates storage recesses. At many points flights of stairs led up to a second floor. The buildings were sturdily built and of a tight-knit urban texture. The network of narrow streets and alleys, connecting small 'squares', suggests a notable degree of organisation and an uncanny similarity of plan to a typical modern Cycladic town.

The movable finds—mostly in the museum in Chora—which are of remarkable quality, include clay storage vases over 1m in height with moulded decorations, conical drinking cups, cooking vessels, and seals. The imported materials and objects in metal and obsidian indicate commercial links with Crete, the nearby smaller islands, and the mainlands of Greece and Asia Minor.

IOS CHORA

Shortly before reaching Chora after the climb from Yialos, the base of the ancient city's **fortification walls of the 6th century** BC is visible in long runs of schist blocks beside the main road, to the left of where the *kalderimi* crosses its course. These walls originally encircled the whole hill above, suggesting that Archaic *Ios* was already a community of some size. It had an enviable location with a panoramic, natural acropolis, overlooking its harbour entrance, a protected civic centre in the saddle below, and an agriculturally productive hinterland a little way to its north. Today's **Chora** climbs attractively up to the rocky peak of the old acropolis, covering the site of the ancient habitation. The broad saddle to the south of the hill (which now lies between the main road and the foot of the hill) has several wells which remain from the ancient settlement. It is likely that the *agora* and the principal public buildings of Ancient *Ios* were located in this well-protected area, close to the sources of water. An *exedra* and other vestiges of Hellenistic and Roman buildings are visible just beside the *Demarcheion* or Town Hall to the south of the main road. The neoclassical building which houses the Town Hall, includes a small **Archaeological Museum** in its ground floor, consisting of two rooms of well-displayed material from the prehistoric period and two from the historic period (open daily 8.30–3, except Mon).

The centre-piece of the collection is the rich and varied material coming from the prehistoric site of Skarkos (*see above*). Many of the smaller items—schematic figurines, cups, seals and metal tools—are exhibited here, as well as several large *pithoi*—some for storage, some for burial: sufficient fragments were found to permit their complete restoration. They constitute some of the best examples of such objects from the 3rd millennium BC. Of particular interest also are the querns and grinders with visible vestiges of red pigment; and a series of oblong stamps bearing clear seal-impressions for clay. There are some fine **Archaic carved *stelai***, probably of Parian workmanship—one of a young warrior who raises his hand to the front of his helmet as if to remove it.

A curious, later *stele* found at Aghia Theodoti, is decorated with two snakes or vipers (one partly coiled) and an **inscription** between them which gives the date of a sacrifice from which it appears that the calendar of Ios included a month called the *Homerea*—named in honour of Homer, who was believed to be buried on the island.

Another pleasing Neoclassical building with porch and pediment, currently abandoned, looks onto the '*agora*' area from the eastern end.

The most important churches of Chora are at the bottom of the acropolis hill. Almost opposite the Town Hall across a stand of trees is **Aghia Ekaterini**, a compact 17th century church, which incorporates several column fragments in its cupola-drum and a piece of Ionic capital in the south wall. The church is believed to stand on the site of the temple of Pythian Apollo, the largest and most important of the island's temples. Immediately to its north sits the long, low structure of the much earlier (possibly 14th century) church of **Aghios Ioannis Prodromos**, with a raised crossed barrel-vault. Abutting it to the north is the island's cathedral of the Evangelismós, built in 1930 to replace an older church on the same spot dedicated to Aghios Nikolaos. 75m to the east of Aghia

Ekaterini, is the domed structure of an abandoned and dilapidated church, known locally as the '**Frangokklisía**', or 'Latin Church'. In similar fashion to Aghia Ekaterini it has blind niches in the octagonal drum below the cupola and in general has the appearance of a typical Byzantine church of the 14th or 15th century, although it is hard to date more exactly in its present condition. Its name implies that it was used principally for the Latin rite by the island's small Catholic community; after this it appears that the church was left unadopted and abandoned.

Above the cathedral church of the Evangelismós the heart of the old chora is bisected, east/west by the main '*calle*' which links Kato and Epano Piatsa, two apologies for squares, between which the main commercial activity of the old town is found. Beside the upper square— 'Epano Piatsa'—is the double church of **Aghios Andreas and Aghia Kyriakí** which incorporates ancient spolia in its interior. At the top of the habitation, just below the rocky crown of the hill is the church of the **Panaghia Kremniótissa**, with a shaded panoramic terrace opening out in front of its west door. From here a path leads up through the rocks towards the summit; the penultimate church, **Aghios Giorgios**, just below the top, has part of a **marble tablet**, densely engraved with early 4th century BC decrees, immured into the south corner of its façade. The summit, now occupied by the chapel of Aghios Nikolaos, was the principal look-out of the ancient acropolis. At the end of the 14th century the Venetian, Marco Crispo built a fortified enclosure here, using ancient foundations where possible; little of it now remains to be seen beyond short breaks of wall.

MYLOPOTAS

Less than a kilometre south by foot from the southeastern corner of Chora is the celebrated **bay of Mylopótas**—a long sweep of pure sand, framed between two headlands. This and Manganari Bay in the south of the island, lie at the heart of the island's fame as a pleasure-resort, and in the 1960s and '70s became places of pilgrimage for a generation of hippies, nudists and hedonists, as well as those who were simply in search of an 'uncorrupted' Greece. The bay takes its name from the watermills which functioned in the gulleys of the seasonal torrents which collected the down-flow from the mountain of Megalo Vouni behind. The unmade track which climbs up from the south end of the bay, joins with the main asphalt road south to Manganari after 5km (*see below*).

Set amongst vegetation on the promontory to the north of the bay and visible from the road as it climbs back to

Chora are two villas, which were built by the painter Yiannis Gaitis (1923–84). The creation of the **Gaitis-Simosi Museum**, under the aegis of Gaitis's daughter, is now in progress: the buildings will become exhibition spaces for modern art, centred around the works of the artist himself. Gaitis's inventive and memorable work is instantly recognisable from its almost obsessive repetition of a characteristic motif—that of the stiff, silhouetted male figures with hat and striped jacket, who often appear in phalanxes. Gaitis discovered Ios together with his close friend Jean-Marie Drot, French author and documentary film-maker: Gaitis designed for Drot the house on the promontory which in turn will be given over to exhibiting Drot's private collection of modern art.

THE NORTH OF THE ISLAND: EPANO KAMBOS & 'HOMER'S TOMB'

The road north from Chora affords good views over the bay of Ormos, with the terraced hill of Skarkos and the excavations on its north slope clearly visible in the foreground. After 5km it descends into **Epano Kambos** ('Upper meadow') which is exactly what its name denotes: a fertile, cultivated area at a height of about 80-100m above sea-level. Watered by the run-off from the hills which surround and protect it from the winds, the area has always constituted the greatest source of agricultural wealth for the island. It is no surprise therefore to find the remains of a **Hellenistic farmstead** in its midst. (*Not easy to locate: coming from Chora, take the first track to the left at the last right-hand bend before the road levels into the floor of the valley. Fork right after 100m. Where the track ends, a walled path leads on towards a small church to the left-hand side, which marks the camouflaged ruins of the ancient building.*) The precisely laid masonry of long blocks of schist, 'ballooned' on their outer face and drafted at their corners, with occasional vertical scoring on some faces, indicates a late Hellenistic date for what must have been a substantial farm building, combining safe-storage and dwelling in one. The doorway on the southwest side tapers to the top, suggesting that it was originally corbelled. A number of the monolithic ceiling blocks still survive, though not in the original configuration.

From the northern end of the Epano Kambos valley, a new road winds through rough and uninhabited terrain towards the tip of the island where, at its northernmost promontory, are the remains of the watchtower of **Psa-**

ropyrgos, and the so-called '**Tomb of Homer**'. The ruined, rectangular tower was well-sited for watching the busy straits between Ios and Herakleia. The site has been considerably altered and reorganised. The masonry of the walls here is not that of a Hellenistic watchtower, but is of a much later construction: it incorporates, however, several articulated and dressed blocks of pure Naxos marble which are clearly ancient and formed the doorframe for an earlier building of some substance. Three of these have been re-assembled in recent times so as create a makeshift shrine for Homer's supposed resting-place: others flank the present entrance.

HOMER AND IOS

The written evidence for Homer's connection with Ios comes principally from Pausanias (*Descrip.* X, 24.2), apart from three words in Pliny (*Hist. Nat.* IV, 69) and a passing reference in Strabo ('according to some writers…', Geog. X, 5.1). The phrases from 'Herodotus's *Life of Homer*, chapter 34', engraved on the marble plaques erected by the municipality at the site, are misleading: no such work of Herodotus exists. A piece of 3rd or 4th century AD literary fiction, written by an anonymous individual referred to today as 'the pseudo-Herodotus' does exist. Since it opens with a lie—stating that it is 'the work of Herodotus' and is 'completely reliable'—it is difficult to accord any of its content credibility. Pausanias, however, writing in the 2nd century AD about the monuments of Delphi, recalls an oracle relating to Homer:

[At Delphi] … you can see a bronze statue of Homer on a slab, and read the oracle that they say Homer received. 'Blessed and unhappy—you were born to be both./You seek your fatherland; but you have no fatherland, only a motherland. / The island of Ios is the fatherland of your mother, and it will receive you /When you are dead; but be on your guard against the riddle of the young children.' The inhabitants of Ios point to Homer's tomb on the island, and in another area to that of Clymene, who was, they say, the mother of Homer.

We do not know—any more than Pausanias who never set foot on Ios—exactly where those tombs he mentions were located on the island.

Already by Hellenistic times, when the island minted coins with the head of Homer on the obverse and the legend 'ΟΜΗΡΟΣ' on the reverse, a strong tradition clearly existed that Homer, on a journey to Athens, was shipwrecked or taken ill on Ios and died there. By the time of Hadrian there was widespread interest in the details of Homer's life, prompting the Emperor himself even to consult the Delphic Oracle on the matter. There are no fewer than ten fictional 'Lives' of the poet known from late Antiquity—not just by the pseudo-Herodotus, but by a pseudo-Plutarch, Proclus and several other anonymous authors.

Homer's greatness was such that any place which could stake some claim to his life or relics could gain prestige and profit thereby. Even in Antiquity, no fewer than seven cities claimed to be his birthplace. And until very recently on Chios, visitors were shown a house in the village of Pitios which was said to be 'Homer's'. In recent times, even though the site to which Pausanias referred was long forgotten, the tradition on Ios clearly needed some physical 'incarnation', and the combined ruins of a tower and a prehistoric grave-yard on this remote promontory nicely

fulfilled that need. The present site was first 'identified' by the Dutch envoy, Count Pasch van Krienen
in 1771, who claimed with romantic flair—100 years
before Schliemann said something similar in respect
of Agamemnon at Mycenae—that as he opened the
grave he had looked for an instant upon the uncorrupted body of Homer, until it decomposed before
his eyes.

THE EAST OF THE ISLAND:
AGHIA THEODOTI, PSATHI &
THE MONASTERY OF AGHIOS IOANNIS

The wild and exposed east coast of the island has the feel
of a remote and largely uninhabited frontier area: the remains of foundations and a surface aqueduct from the
Roman period, in the coastal area between **Aghia Theodóti** (10km) and Psáthi (17.5km), suggest that it was more
inhabited in antiquity however. The church of Aghia Theodóti, set above the wide bay of that name 5.5km east of
the road junction above Epano Kambos, is an unusual

piece of 16th century architecture: its broad interior, preceded by a shallow transverse narthex, develops beneath two successive, large domes, creating a pleasing effect. The annexes and areas to the west were added to host the eating and dancing in honour of the Saint, which takes place on 8 September in what is one of the most popular feasts of the year for Ios.

Between Aghia Theodoti and Psáthi, the road climbs high into the mountainous interior, once covered with the oak forests from which Ios formerly derived considerable wealth. At 12.5km from Chora, just before the road begins to descend again to Psathi, a detour of 4.5km leads right (south), past the heavily restored church of Aghios Giorgios, to the 16th century '**monastery of *Pyrgos***' dedicated to Aghios Ioannis Pródromos (St John the Baptist), built on a panoramic ledge, just below the highest summit of the island (713m). From this vantage point, the entire north of the island, and Sikinos and Folegandros across the water, are laid out as if on a map. Although there is no visual evidence on site to corroborate it, local tradition claims that the monastery was built on the site of a temple of Apollo which, if it did exist, would have vied with that at Bassae for its lofty and dramatic position. It is more probable that the site was occupied by an ancient watch-tower. The fortified quadrangle of monastic buildings is now ruined, but the church which has a free-cross design with semi-domes on the lateral arms is well-maintained and has a pleasing interior space.

Descending to the coast towards Psathi, the main road passes the ruins of the Venetian castle of **Palaiokastro**, visible on the summit ahead, before the road turns sharply east (*15 mins by path and steps, from the bend at 14km*).

The visible ruins and existing masonry in a local limestone— a single enceinte of walls, enclosing an irregular space on the edge of a precipitous drop—appear to date from around 1500, even though there is some suggestion that a smaller Byzantine fortress was built on the site over three centuries earlier. Once the Venetian Pisani family had taken over control of the island from the Crispo family in 1450, a need was clearly felt to expand the defences and surveillance capabilities of the island beyond the area of Chora to this eastern seaboard. The site here overlooks a vitally important maritime route, connecting both Rhodes and Crete with Naxos and the Western Aegean. Remains of a cistern and of several buildings survive within the enceinte. The church of the **Panaghia Palaiokastrítissa** dates from the late 17th century.

The road ends at Psáthi (17.5km) a remote and relatively exposed bay, which appears to have known greater significance in antiquity than it does today. An Ionic temple to **Poseidon** *Phytalmios* ('the Nourisher') stood here, on the site now occupied by the church of **Aghios Nikolaos**, also known locally as the Panaghia 'tou Pori' (*not far in from the coast, 400m southeast of the village; marked by a palm tree*). The high podium built of eroded schists is visible below the north side of the church: other spolia lie in the vicinity.

The beach of Psathi, together with the others along the island's central eastern coast, constitute a breeding habitat for the **Mediterranean sea-turtle**. To the north of the bay, on the island of Psathónisi, the remains of an Early Cycladic settlement have been identified.

THE SOUTH OF THE ISLAND

The southern extremity of the island is a landscape quite different from the centre and north, and no less dramatic. Its interior has only recently become accessible by the building of a surfaced road which leads down to the southern tip of the island (*Either 25km from Chora—metalled all the way—by taking the road via Epano Kambos, towards Psathi, and branching south at the junction at 10.5km; or 18km—partially unmade—via Mylopotas).* On the south side of the island's central mountain-massif the scenery suddenly changes from long slopes covered in mountain scrub to **an eroded and boulder-strewn landscape** of often strange and jagged forms, similar in nature to that around Volax on Tinos or Manganitis on Ikaria, produced by a combination of violent volcanic activity and constant wind erosion. Hidden in an oasis of scattered trees in the midst of this landscape is the **monastery of Aghios Ioannis Prodromos of Kalamos**. Never was a dedication to the Baptist more appropriate than in this desert landscape which unexpectedly yields water here. Before the monastery was founded at the turn of the 19th century, the site must originally have been occupied by a hermitage—reminiscent in setting of the those of the early Desert Fathers.

At this point, the road divides east to the sandy beach of Kalamos on the east coast, or south to the double ***bay of Manganári**, site of a flourishing settlement of the Early Cycladic period. The view from the descending road of this broad and gentle bay, its two shallow sweeps of virgin sand separated by an outcrop of reefs, with the plain and the mountains behind and the island of Santorini ahead across the water, is one of the loveliest in the Cyclades.

PRACTICAL INFORMATION

840 01 **Ios**: area 108 sq.km; perimeter 87km; resident population 1,862; max. altitude 714 m. **Port Authority**: T. 22860 91264. **Travel information**: Acteon Travel (T. 22860 91343, fax 91088, www.acteon.gr). **General information**: www.iosgreece.com

ACCESS

Although the island has no airport, it has one or more daily connections to Piraeus either by regular ferry (8–10 hours) or by high-speed vessel (4½ hours). Ios is also a terminus of the route operated by *SAOS Ferries* from Santorini and Anafi, via Sikinos and Folegandros, offering connections with these lesser islands five times weekly. In the summer there are also fast links almost daily with Santorini and Naxos by *Flying Dolphin*.

LODGING

Modern, welcoming, comfortable and with a wide range of services, is the **Liostasi Spa Hotel** (*T. 22860 92140, fax 92680, www.liostasi.gr*) situated panoramically between the port and Chora. At the north end of Ormos Bay, are **Petra Villas**—attractively appointed studios, in relative quiet and seclusion, close to the water (*T. 22860 91409*).

EATING

The challenge on Ios is locating simple and genuine Greek cuisine: in the main centres this can be found at **Taverna Susanna** in Plateia Limaniou beside the port, and at the small **Koutouki tou Saïni**, near the 'Epano Piatsa' at the eastern end of the old part of Chora. For good fresh fish, vegetable dishes and salads, the **Taverna Alonistra** at Psáthi on the east coast of the island is reliable and pleasant.

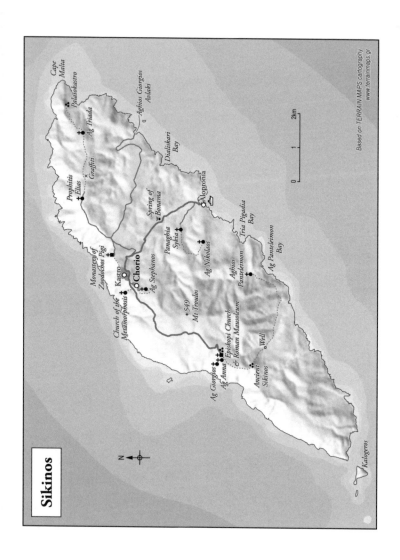

Sikinos

SIKINOS

The traditions that the island's former name was '*Oenoe*', from the fame of its wine ('*οἶνος*'), and that its founder-hero, Sikinos, was the grandson of Dionysos, are reflected in the excellent local wine that the island still produces from its remaining vineyards. It can be found in local *tavernas* and is at its freshest in the early summer months. It is not a sophisticated wine, but in its strong, orange-pink colour and salty flavour it represents a true and centuries-old tradition of wine-making in the Greek Islands which is now rapidly disappearing. It must approximate in flavour to the quasi-fortified wines which the ancients drank diluted with water. Sikinos was also praised for its figs in Antiquity: vines and figs were the only plants hardy enough to survive in its harsh, rocky landscape. Its inhabitants had to be equally tenacious and hardy to survive on the island: the two known settlements of antiquity, at Palaiokastro on the island's eastern extremity, and Ancient *Sikinos* in the southwest of the island, are both remarkable for the alarming perpendicularity of their sites—marvellously panoramic, but tough indeed to inhabit. It is no surprise that the island, which had no good harbour and was therefore frequently rendered inaccessible for long periods by the winds, became a by-word for obscurity and insignificance in the metropolitan world of ancient Athens.

It is all the more remarkable, therefore, that one of the most interesting and best-preserved Roman monuments in the Cyclades is to be found on Sikinos—a grand mausoleum, of oriental inspiration, originally thought to have been a temple, which has survived by being converted into a Christian church dedicated to the Dormition of the Virgin and is now known as the monastery of Episkopí. This singular, and in many ways moving, monument underlines the need to reassess the significance of small, island-outposts such as Sikinos in the period of Roman occupation. We know too little about their life and uses at such times.

To be so close to the pulsating life of Ios, Sikinos is a remarkably tranquil island with much of its mountainous landscape wild and scarcely accessible—ideal for walking and for observing birds of passage in spring and autumn. The island has several interesting rural churches in which fragmentary wall-paintings still survive; and a handful of secluded coves with sandy margins, clear water and a rich underwater life.

HISTORY & LEGEND

According to legend (Apollonius of Rhodes, *Argonautica* I. 622 ff.), Hypsipyle saved her father, Thoas, son of Dionysos and Ariadne, from the massacre of all the males on the island of Lemnos perpetrated by the Lemnian women in revenge for the supposed unfaithfulness of their menfolk, by putting him in a wooden chest and throwing him into the sea. The chest came ashore at Sikinos which at that time bore the name '*Oenoe*'. Thoas sired by the Nymph Neïda a child named 'Sikinos', in honour of whom the island's name was changed. Elements of the legend hint at a possible Mycenaean settlement of the island. The island was later colonised by mainland Dorians, but received much Ionian influence from its neighbours.

The first historical mention of Sikinos is a comment reportedly made by Solon that he would 'rather be someone from Sikinos than fail in his duty to Athens'—implying that to have the misfortune of coming from Sikinos was something akin to living in utter oblivion. In 425 BC the island was assessed at a yearly tribute of 1,000 drachmas in the lists of the Athenian League—the lowest assessment of any island; in 378 BC it joined the Second Athenian Alliance. Coins minted for Sikinos in the 3rd century BC display the head of Dionysos or bunches of grapes, reflecting the age-old association of the island with viticulture.

Because of a lack of references in literature and epigraphy to the island, it has always been assumed that it simply functioned as a place of political exile in Roman times, but the grandeur of edifices such as the mausoleum at Episkopi suggest a more complex reality for the island in the Imperial period.

Along with its neigbours, Sikinos became part of the Latin Duchy of Naxos in 1207 under Marco Sanudo, but was briefly re-taken for Byzantium by the Veronese admiral Licario in 1276. It eventually came under Ottoman control in 1566. The church and Roman ruin at Episkopi was first observed and admired by the Dutchman, Count Pasch van Krienen in 1771; it was documented by the German scholar, Ludwig Ross, in 1837; and visited by James Theodore Bent in 1884. In 1828, Sikinos was incorporated into the Greek State. The island was occupied by Italian forces from 1941–43 during the Second World War. Electricity was first brought to the island only in 1974.

AROUND ALOPRONIA

Nature left both Folegandros and Sikinos as fortresses in the sea with steep slopes and cliffs at almost every point on their perimeters. The harbour of Aloprónia or 'Ano Prónoia', in the middle of the south coast, is the only concession to a partially sheltered approach on Sikinos: even so it is exposed to the strong winds that drive from the south across the Cretan Sea and can leave the island inaccessible for days on end. The inlet has an attractive, sandy beach and a valley of relative fertility stretching behind it, watered by the **spring of Bonamá** which rises beside the road, 1.4km to the north of the shore, at the foot of the steep rise leading to the ridge of the island. The spring was a rarity for an island that had otherwise to exist on wells and stored rainwater. High up on eminences to the west overlooking the valley are two of the oldest churches on the island, both of which contain vestiges of late mediaeval painting, suggesting that the island knew some prosperity in the 14th century. The easiest to reach is the church of the **Panaghia 'Sykia'**, which is a 30-minute walk up the track leading steeply to the northwest from the main road, just north of the port. The low undulating structure of the church, with a high belfry over its west door, sits on an outcrop of unusual and attractively brecciated pink rock. It is a simple barrel-vaulted, single-aisle structure with a transverse narthex. Along its south exterior are two deep vaulted niches which would appear to be the *arcosolia* of important tombs. The church dates from the 14th century, and the patches of attractive, but unsophisticated **wall-painting** in its interior date from shortly after. They are painted in strong earth-colours: the *Presentation of the Virgin* can be clearly seen on the north side and, to the south, the figures of saints—*Aghios Merkourios* and others. Around the church are the remains of a small settlement, indicating that it was once the centre of a small monastic community. Visible on the next hill-crest to the south is the small church of **Aghios Nikolaos**, dating from the first years of the 14th century, which also contains similarly fragmentary wall-painting. Though close as the crow flies, the church can only be approached by a long sweep west around the head of the ravine, which takes the best part of 40 minutes.

Along the coast from Aloprónia, are a couple of tiny and secluded coves for bathing, accessible by foot: Dial-iskari (45 mins) to the northeast, and Aghios Panteleimon (90 mins) to the southwest across the ridge of the Ráches Katérgou. Both have clear water, shingle beaches, but little or no shade.

KASTRO & CHORA

After passing the spring of Bonamá, the road from the port rises steeply to the island's main settlement (4km from Aloprónia), which beetles along a ridge overlooking the cliffs of the north coast. The habitation divides into two settlements: Chora or Chorió on the slope to the southwest, and Kastro to the east. The configuration of the settlement is remarkably similar to that on Folegandros: a 300m drop straight to the sea on the north side, a large church overlooking from the hill to the east, and a mediaeval *kastro* at the heart of the settlement. The effect however is less intimate on Sikinos because of the lack of an obvious 'centre', which here is constituted by a loose network of pergola-shaded streets just to the north of the main church of the Pantanassa. Entering **Kastro** from the saddle between the two communities (i.e. from the southwest), a low tunnel-like entrance—the '**Paraporti**' or postern gate—leads into an open square which was the central area of the mediaeval fortified unit, built during the second half of the 15th century along lines similar to the *kastro* settlements on Siphnos, Kimolos, Antiparos and Folegandros. The blank, rear walls of the houses formed the exterior enceinte of the *kastro*, while their façades faced onto the central area. A number of the houses are uninhabited, some are community offices, and a dearth of cafés and eateries in the square leaves what is otherwise an elegant public space somewhat lifeless. At its centre is the church of the Timíos Stavrós, generally referred to as the **Panaghia Pantanassa**, rebuilt in the 18th century, perhaps on the site of an earlier church. The upper floors of the surrounding buildings show the external signs of noble residences—door and window frames in marble, carved with vine-motifs or embellished with rectangular grooves and cornices. In the southwest corner, on the upper floor above the community offices, is a small **Byzantine Museum** (*open July–mid-Sept 10–1*). It includes an interesting photographic display of the principal Byzantine chapels on Sikinos, and a collection of **icons** from the 17th century and after: these include works by the painter of the Cretan-Venetian school, Antonios Skordilis from Milos as well as beautiful examples of carved and gilded wooden **sanctuary-doors**, painted with the *Annunciation* and *Apostles*.

To the southwest of Kastro lies **Chorió**, which blends at its eastern extremity into an area of ruined houses further up the hill. It is separated from Kastro by the main road and the long, symmetrical **neoclassical school-building** put up in the first decade of the 20th century. Although Chorió, with its steep and narrow alleys, dates from sub-

stantially earlier, the main church in its lower area is a lu-
minous building of the 17th century. The only Byzantine
church is **Aghios Stephanos**, which dates from the 14th
century and lies outside the village, 10 minutes by foot to
the south. There is a small **Folklore Museum** in Chorió,
exhibiting olive-presses, looms, ceramics and other domestic and agricultural artefacts from the island's recent
history.

Clearly visible from Chorió is the winding path which
leads up the mountain east of Kastro to the **monastery
of the Zoödochos Pigi**. About half way up the path is the
small, vaulted, stone chapel of the Panaghia Pantochará
(currently being built) which is dedicated to the memory
of the poet Odysseas Elytis (1911–96), for whom the islands of the Southern Cyclades and their wide panoramas
were a constant source of inspiration. The path ends at
the monastery, which is dedicated to the Virgin as the
'Life-giving Fount'. (*Access to the interior is only regularly
possible at around 6–6.30 pm every day, when a lady from
the village opens up the catholicon to service the oil-lamps.*)
With a position strongly reminiscent of the church of the
Panaghia on Folegandros, the Zoödochos Pigi is built
uncompromisingly like a fortress and was designed to
provide a last refuge for the islanders when under attack. Inside, an esplanade with a well precedes the broad

façade of the church: to the north a low parapet protects the space from the precipice beyond. The ruined buildings of the monastery, which was abandoned in 1834, surround the *catholicon*; the staircases, baking ovens and door thresholds are still visible. The interior of the church is relatively plain apart from the highly ornate **tombstone of Dionysios Protopsaltis** which lies prominently in the middle of the central aisle, carved with floral motifs and the double-headed eagle of Byzantium. Protopsaltis was the benefactor of the monastery when it was founded in 1690.

EPISKOPI & THE SOUTHWEST OF THE ISLAND

Just outside Chorió and Kastro, to the north of the road as it heads west, is the church of the **Metamorphosis**, or Transfiguration, which stands among pine and almond trees beside a turreted neoclassical house, sited on the very edge of the north cliffs of the island; the combination of the view, the peace, the vegetation and the different styles of building make this one of the most enchanting spots on the island. The church has origins which go back to the 14th or 15th century, though it appears to have been restored in the 17th century. The steps outside the southeast corner of the church are re-used architraves: the decorative carving on them is identical to that on some of the door and window frames found on the buildings in the square of the Kastro.

Beyond the church of the Metamorphosis, the newly constructed road clings to the barren west slope of Mount Troullos (549m), the island's highest peak, following the route of the old paved *kalderimi* which runs nearby, and offering good views to Paros, Antiparos, Siphnos, Kimolos and Milos. The route was described by Theodore Bent in 1884 as 'lined with immense fig-trees and extensive vineyards, showing the fertility of the place'. The road ends (5km from Chorió) a short distance by foot from the *church of the Episkopí, which is visible ahead in the middle of a wild and open valley ringed by mountains and ravines—solitary, like an apparition. This is one of the most unusual buildings in the Cyclades: a well-preserved, 2nd or 3rd century AD, Roman construction, subsequently adapted into a church dedicated to the Dormition of the Virgin and set in an unblemished landscape of natural grandeur. Visible ahead to the south is the peak of Aghia Marina (444m), crowned by a small white chapel and the remains of mediaeval fortification: this was the acropolis of Ancient *Sikinos* whose ruins are scattered down the slope below; the area where the church of the

Episkopí now stands was the cemetery area, below and outside the ancient city.

The building

The path leads to the rear side of the building, where the protruding apse of the church can be seen, as well as the outline of two successive roof-vaults above. As far up as the distinctive **cornice**, the masonry is Ancient Roman—perfectly preserved along the sides and at the corners. Above the cornice, surrounding the 17th century dome, is rough masonry added later to act as a fortification. Theodore Bent was told when he visited in 1884 that monks had used this area on the roof as a refuge when besieged by pirates. The southeast corner shows the beginning of the original pediment, indicating that the Roman structure originally had the form of a pedimented temple. From the two columns that flank the front entrance to the church at rakish angles, it becomes clear that the Roman structure had the design of a **di-style in antis temple**, i.e with two columns (c. 10m high) between two flanks which supported the frontal trabeation and pediment. The spaces between these elements have been filled in with rough, improvised masonry. The roughly cubic form and considerable height in proportion to the width link the building to structures of a similar design in the East of the Roman empire—in Syria, and at Diocaesarea in southeast-

ern Turkey, for example. There is no sign of an ancient altar before the entrance, but instead a deep rock-cut **cistern**,
roofed with large stone slabs. Another cistern lies just to the
north. Large pieces of the magnificent, 'dog-tooth' or dentil-
lated cornice are built into the improvised wall opposite the
entrance.

It seems unlikely that the building was actually a temple,
even though there is a strong tradition dating from the visit
in 1837 of the German archaeologist, Ludwig Ross, who first
designated the building as a 'temple to Pythian Apollo' on
the basis of a now lost inscription in the vicinity. Its south-
westerly orientation is unsuitable for cult, and it is built in
an area which appears clearly to have been a cemetery and to
have possessed other funerary monuments (*see below*). More
probably, it was a temple-like '***heroön***' or **mausoleum** to an
important individual, similar to those found frequently in
the eastern areas of the Empire. This interpretation raises
its own problems, however: Sikinos has generally been con-
sidered to have been used by Rome as a place of exile for
political undesirables during the period of the Empire. Who,
then, on Sikinos in the 2nd century AD could afford or merit
a monument of such grand proportions?

The history

Masonry and design suggest that the building is unlikely

to date from before the second half of the 2nd century AD. For it to have survived so well into later times, it must early on have been converted into a Christian church—perhaps even as early as the 6th century. At that point the adaptation was probably minimal; the apse dates from several centuries later. The belfry, drum and cupola are additions of the 17th century—the period in which the height of the main vault also seems to have been altered and the buttressing added on the south side. The grandeur of the building made it an obvious choice for an episcopal seat—hence its current name of 'Episkopí'. The building was recently deconsecrated, and the interior is now bare and filled with wooden scaffolding to support the precariousness of the structure.

Around the church

In addition to the vestigial remains of monastic outbuildings, two 14th century chapels have survived to the north of the building: **Aghia Anna**, beside the church's north wall, which has remains of **wall-paintings** in the apse and along the north and south walls; the other, **Aghios Giorgios**, further up the hill, where the paintings are better conserved, with the donors who commissioned them also depicted. The fabric of the walls includes several ancient blocks.

Two hundred and fifty metres southwest of the church of the Episkopi is a deconsecrated, barrel-vaulted chapel:

below its southeast corner, an outcrop of natural rock has been neatly cut into three steps and a square recess for the **pedestal of a funerary monument**. It would appear that this whole area was a cemetery, dominated by the mausoleum to the northeast. The area lay outside the inhabited city and overlooked the small patch of fertile land which must have provisioned the city's inhabitants.

A thirty-minute walk to the southwest towards the peak of Aghia Marina brings you to the site of **Ancient *Sikinos***. The habitation occupied a triangular area bounded by a fortress at the summit of Aghia Marina (where the chapel now stands); a shoulder to the northeast of it where there are the remains of fortification; and another shoulder to the east where there is a clear platform for a public or sacred building which stood on the ridge looking down to the shore to the southeast. In the concavity between these three points are the remains of retaining walls and a fortified enceinte constructed in masonry of small dimensions. The site is almost impracticably steep and drops straight into the gorge below where there is a wellhead—perhaps formerly a spring. On the slope can be seen two lime-kilns, now abandoned, once used for reducing marble to mortar: this may explain why there is little marble left on the site itself. From the wellhead—known locally as the *Pigádi Mánali*—paths lead to the remote chapels of the wild southwestern extremity of the island: east to Aghios Panteleimon (90 mins); south to Aghios Ioannis (70 mins) on the coast; and southwest to Aghios Spyridon (90 mins), overlooking the islets in the strait between Folegandros and Sikinos.

THE NORTHEAST OF THE ISLAND

From a point c. 500 m east of Kastro, 5km of newly-completed road has been driven east through the landscape, down to the tiny beach and inlet of **Aghios Giorgios Avlaki**. At present there is nothing more than the chapel of St George and the beautiful bay; but it is intended that a new resort for the island be created here in the future. By continuing northwards from the point (1km east of Kastro) where the new road branches downhill to the east, you follow the ridge of the hills for a further 1.5km until the track ends at the chapel of Prophitis Elias. From here a path leads east to Cape Málta at the eastern extremity of the island: the 230m high, south face of it promontory is occupied by the island's other main archaeological site, known as **Palaiokastro**. Surface finds here suggest that there was settlement in the Early Bronze Age (3rd millennium BC). Most visible today however, are the remains

of ancient and Byzantine habitation across the precipitous slope—which, if anything, is even steeper and more
exposed than that of Ancient *Sikinos*. It appears that the
ancients on this island relished inaccessibility and the ex-
citement of living on preposterous gradients. (*The walk is
a minimum 2½ hour round-trip from Prophitis Elias. The
path is clear at first: then, by following the highest contours,
you pass the chapel of Aghia Triada, and thence descend to
the narrow neck of the promontory.*)

On the low rise in the path beyond the first dip after
leaving Prophitis Elias, two rocks with smooth faces have
curious **graffiti** carved in them, which must date from the
early 19th century: they figure two superimposed, quite
carefully drawn sailing ships bearing the flag of the Greek
Revolution and inscribed '*IEΔ*'. Engraved more deeply
are what look like two Arabic initials—the letter '*lām*' (ل),
twice in succession.

From a distance the bases of buildings, terracing and
retaining walls across the upper reaches of the south slope
of the promontory can be seen: these are composed of
compact, roughly hewn and squared blocks. Just beyond
the neck of the promontory at the western end of the inhabited area is a deep cleft in the rock which appears to
have been adapted into a natural cistern for water-collec-
tion. At the opposite end, quantities of fallen rubble-ma-

sonry end abruptly at the eastern perimeter of the settlement, which is clearly delimited, running down from the
saddle between the two peaks of the promontory. What
this mountain-clinging community must have done for a
passable harbour, or even for drinking-water during the
long summer months, is not clear; but their panoramic
position meant that no maritime traffic south from the
islands of Naxos and Ios (both clearly visible on the hori-
zon) escaped their attention.

PRACTICAL INFORMATION

840 10 Sikinos: area 41 sq.km; perimeter 40km; resident population 238; max. altitude 549m. **Port Authority**: T. 22860 51222. **Information**: Koundouris Travel, T. 22860 51168.

ACCESS

To reach Sikinos, it is generally necessary to change ferries at Ios or Santorini. Direct connections to Athens are only twice weekly with *G.A. Ferries* (from Piraeus), and once a week with *NEL Lines* (from Lavrion). Throughout the summer, however, there are connections by regular ferry (*SAOS Lines*) to Ios and Santorini five times weekly.

LODGING

The most comfortable hotel on Sikinos—the **Hotel Porto Sikinos**—with pleasantly appointed rooms, is in the port of Aloprónia (*T. 22860 51220, fax 51247, www.portosikinos. gr*). In the chora, simpler, family-run furnished rooms with marvellous sunset views can be found at the '**Iliovasilema**' (*T./fax 22860 51173, www. sikinos-sunset.gr*): attached to it, is a good patisserie (for Greek sweets principally) run by the same family.

EATING

Klimatari, just north of the main church of Kastro, has simple Greek fare, some local cheese at certain periods, and delicious *Sikiniot wine. The fresh wine can be cloudy and, like the best island wines, tastes slightly salty. It alone merits the journey to Sikinos.

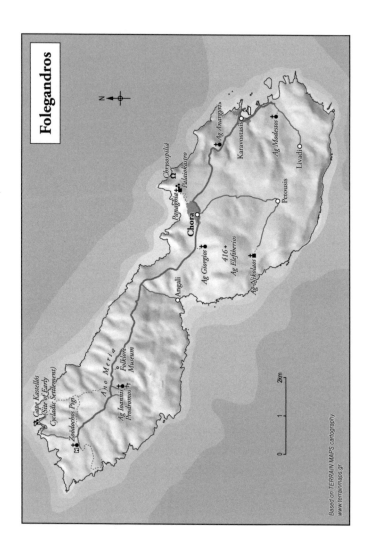

Folegandros

N

Cape Kastellis
(Site of Early
Cycladic Settlement)

Zoodochos Pigi

Ano Meria

Ag Ioannis
Prodromos

Folklore
Museum

Angali

Ag Giorgios

416
Ag Eleftherios

Ag Nikolaos

Chora

Panaghia

Chrysospilia
Palaiokastro

Ag Anargyris

Karavostasis

Petousis

Ag Modestos

Livadi

Based on TERRAIN MAPS cartography
www.terrainmaps.gr

0   1   2km

FOLEGANDROS

Approaching the island in an evening of February 1884, when the world's skies still possessed the lurid sunset colour given them by the eruption of Krakatoa six months previously, James Theodore Bent felt that of 'all the islands of the Aegean Sea, Pholygandros can boast of the most majestic coastline; in fact', he claimed, 'I doubt it can be equalled anywhere'. The island is indeed somewhat like a wall or wind-break in the sea with dramatic cliffs on all sides except on the east, opposite Sikinos, where they relent sufficiently to allow for a small harbour and an apron of fertile land. Few islands furthermore can boast a more dramatically sited, yet attractive, Chora than Folégandros. It possesses a compact mediaeval centre and a chain of beautiful, shaded squares. What surprises is that it feels so gracious and reassuring when one is inside it, unaware of its dramatic position on the edge of a two hundred metre drop to the sea.

Folégandros is a delightful island which has deservedly begun to receive a faithful and discerning tourism. It has several civilised places to stay, pleasant cafés, many attractive beaches and a number of interesting walks along the island's network of stone-paved mule paths. Contrasting pleasantly with any detectable preciosity in the island's beautiful *Chora*, are the widely dispersed settlements of Ano Meriá along the island's western plateau where an unaffected, rural life continues centred around a centuries-old tradition of husbandry and agriculture.

The island's most interesting archaeological site is unfortunately also its most inaccessible. The cave of Chrysospiliá—which takes its name of the 'Golden Cave' from the colouring of the iron oxides present in the rocks around its entrance—is at the foot of a sheer wall of rock in the north coast which rises 300m above its entrance. The approach by boat is difficult unless the sea is very calm. Apart from the interest of the chambers of stalactites and stalagmites in its interior, its walls are covered in places with names and phrases, incised or written in pigment in the 4th and 3rd centuries BC, when the grotto with its phallic stalactite-formations appears to have been the focus of a curious ephebic cult.

HISTORY

The first evidence of human settlement on the island, at its northern extremity of Kastellos Point, dates from the Early Cycladic II period (mid-3rd millennium BC). Continuity during the Middle and Late Bronze Age (2nd millennium

BC) is indicated by surface finds near the port of Karavostasis and on Palaiokastro Hill, which is where settlement later concentrated in historic times. It is in this period that the island may have acquired its name from the Phoenician '*phelek-gundari*', meaning 'rocky land'; though it was also known to the Greeks, according to Strabo (*Geog.* X, 5.1), by the epithet '*σιδηρείη*' ('like iron') because of the hardness of its terrain. The island was colonised by Dorians, though later received much Ionian influence, eventually developing an Ionian dialect in Hellenistic times. It was assessed to pay a tribute of 2,000 drachmas into the First Athenian League in 425 BC. Most of the visible remains on the island, such as the retaining wall in the cemetery of Chora and the inscriptions in the cave of Chrysospilia, date from the Hellenistic and Roman period however. Folégandros appears briefly to have minted its own coins in the 2nd century BC.

The 12th century Arab geographer, Al-Idrisi, mentions the island by the name '*Belikendra*'. The island was taken by Marco Sanudo into the Duchy of Naxos in 1207 and passed to the Bolognese overlords of Kythnos, the Gozzadini family, in 1336. Although Cristoforo Buondelmonti in his *Liber Insularum* described Folégandros as virtually uninhabited when he visited in c. 1417, the island appears later to have been re-settled from Crete in the 16th century. The Ottoman Empire took complete possession of the island from descendants of the Gozzadini in 1617. In 1715 it suffered a punitive Turkish raid, leaving it once again depopulated. Between 1770 and 1774 it came under Russian rule along with the other Cyclades during the Russo-Turkish war. In 1828 it joined the newly, independent Greek State. In 1918, 1926, 1936, and again in the 1960's the island was used as a place of exile for the political undesirables of the moment. Electricity was only brought to Folégandros in 1974.

FOLEGANDROS CHORA

The *Chora of Folégandros—one of the best preserved and most dramatically sited in the Aegean—divides into two areas: the older, semi-fortified, mediaeval *Kastro* to the north; and the settlement of the 17th and later centuries, contiguous with it, to the south. On the north side cliffs drop 200m almost sheer into the sea below; and to the east, above the church of the Panaghia, is the peak of Palaiokastro which rises to 353m above sea level. The up-

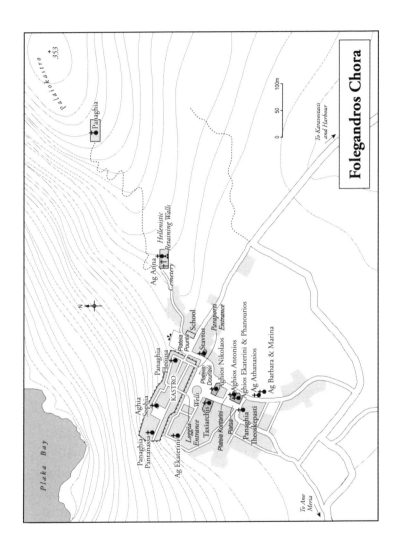

Folegandros Chora

Palaiokastro
+ 353

Panaghia

100m

50

0

To Karavostasis
and Harbour

Hellenistic
Retaining Walls

Ag Anna

Cemetery

N

School

Panaporti
Entrance

Plateia
Pounta

Stavros

Aghios Nikolaos

Panaghia
Eleousa

Aghios Antonios

Aghios Ekaterini & Phanourios

Plateia
Dounavi

KASTRO

Aghia
Sophia

Wells

Ag Athanasios

Ag Barbara & Marina

Entrance

Loggia

Taxiarchis

Panaghia
Pantanassa

Plateia Kontarini

Plateia

Ag Ekaterini

Panaghia
Theoskepasti

Plaka Bay

To Ano
Meria

per slopes of the steep cliff to the northwest of Chora are terraced and cultivated wherever possible, taking advantage of the moisture of their northern exposure, whereas the dry, undulating valley to the southwest is simply walled for goat pasture. Even as late as the 17th century, Folégandros was well-wooded and exported its timber to other Aegean islands. That vegetation was gone within a hundred years. Since the island is particularly steep and rocky, obtaining water and produce subsequently became even more arduous for the island's inhabitants.

All transportation stops at or before **Plateia Pounta**— so named for its position on a ledge-like eminence with an impressive view from its parapet. Facing onto it from the south is the island's neoclassical primary school building (1908) and a small war memorial to its east. Beyond the attractive 19th century church of the **Stavros** in the south corner, with its unusual hexagonal cupola-drum, **Plateia Dounavi** ('Danube'), the main centre of the *chora* and the first of a loose-knit series of squares, lies just to the southwest. The square is an intimate space, attractively paved and gathered around a circular, low-walled dip with two 18th century wells and a welcome stand of plane, lime and acacia trees. The opposite (south) side of the square is bounded by the island's principal church of **Aghios Nikolaos**, which has an interesting, carved throne and iconostasis in its interior; to its west is the early 17th century church of the **Taxiarch**, whose façade is embellished by a *bifora* window with a carved marble pilaster. The north side of the square is constituted by the south wall of the ***Kastro***, which has two entrances—the wider, stepped '*Loggia*' to the west, and the narrower '*Paraporti*' which leads out of Plateia Dounavi at the eastern end of the wall.

As on Antiparos, Kimolos and Siphnos, the *Kastro* is a mediaeval settlement in which the houses face inwards and their outside walls form the 'fortified' enceinte. To the north, the rock precipice forms an effective natural defence; the houses had no lime-plaster in earlier times, and were indistinguishable from the natural rock when seen from a distance. Begun in the early years of Venetian domination, it could accommodate almost 200 families within its small—but not cramped—perimeter. The houses have been remarkably well-preserved without resorting visibly to modern materials; where the buildings cross the tiny alleyways, the passages are roofed with cypress and schist blocks; and the characteristic wooden balconies and parallel flights of steps (especially in the '*Kato Roua*', the first street to left) have survived unaltered. At either end of the upper street, or '*Piso Roua*' are two compact, late-Mediaeval churches—**Aghia Sophia** (west) and the **Panaghia Eleousa** (east)—the latter marked by a fragment of fluted ancient column by its door. Projecting on an outcrop at the western extremity of Kastro, with an unforgettable view, is the church of the **Panaghia Pantanassa**, built by a Cretan immigrant shortly before the end of the 17th century: he appears, kneeling, in the *predella* of the painting on the south sanctuary-door of the screen.

Plateia Dounavi runs south into **Plateia Kontarini**, and thence into a square simply known as '*Piatsa*': in the constantly changing shapes and delightful vistas of these open spaces, the churches appear as islands. Plateia Kontarini is dominated by the façade of the 17th century church of **Aghios Antonios** (restored in 1709) with its fine marble door-frame, vivaciously carved by a local artist: there is more such 'folk-art' in the painted pillars which flank the screen in the church's interior. Further to the south, the '*Piatsa*' is looked onto by the ruined church of the **Panaghia Theoskepastí**. The attractive form of the belfry and the marble door- and window-frames suggest that this was once a fine early-17th century structure; but its interior is now roofless. To the south from here several streets lead out from the centre towards the road to the northwest of the island passing substantial but modestly designed, stone houses built in the 19th century by Folegandriots who had lived and worked in Egypt: the last on the left, before the asphalt road, displays a carved, **ancient grave-*stele*** over its door.

CHURCH OF THE PANAGHIA

To the left of the primary school building overlooking Pounta Square a street leads into the stepped path which winds up to the church of the Panaghia, below the summit of the hill to the east. As you approach the first bend, the **Roman marble bust** of a robed male figure comes into view, erected above an arch in the modern cemetery wall ahead: it gives an intimation that this is the heart of the area occupied by the settlement of Ancient *Pholegandros*. The clearest evidence of this is the long stretch of **Hellenistic retaining wall** inside the cemetery enclosure (*second level, back left*) on which the chapel of Aghia Anna sits. The face of the wall is bisected transversely by a carefully executed 'rope-course' of masonry, which separates the courses of 'ballooning' stone blocks below, from the flatter more finished masonry above. The wall must date from the late 4th or early 3rd century BC. Further up the hill and in the surrounding area are the vestigial remains of ancient habitation. The **church of the Panaghia** itself may occupy the site of a pagan place of worship, which in turn was replaced by an Early Christian church. As you enter the forecourt, some plain ancient column-fragments and **statue bases** can be seen: one of the latter still preserves the tips of the bronze feet of a (probably Roman) statue which stood on it, with the lead filling still visible within the toes. Above, embedded in the lower south wall of the bell-tower, is the robed torso of a **Roman funerary statue** in marble. The church itself dates from c. 1820, when it was rebuilt to replace an earlier 17th century church to which the carved marble west door-frame and the inscription just to the right of the entrance belonged. Inside the spacious interior, the iconostasis and the throne in a grey-white, Tiniot marble, are the work of the sculptor from Tinos, Konstantinos Kaparias.

PALAIOKASTRO & CHRYSOSPILIA

The summit above the church of the Panaghia, known as **Palaiokástro**, functioned successively as the acropolis of Ancient *Pholegandros* and as a fortress in Byzantine and Venetian times. Only the amorphous ruins of mostly later mediaeval walls, some ancient foundations and a scatter of pottery remain to be seen on the site: the view over the island and towards Milos and Siphnos is particularly fine, however. To both west and east the mountain drops almost sheer into the sea 350m below. Far down the east slope, at a height of only 20m above the water is the deep *cave of Chrysospiliá, which is accessible only from the water—and then only in exceptionally calm weather. At times, it is also closed because of excavations in progress. (*The cave is of particular interest and any opportunity when it is possible to visit it should not be missed: this is most easily done as part of a 'round-island' boat-tour in the summer. Call 'Diaplous' tours, T. 22860 41158 for information.*) Improvised concrete steps lead from the rocks at the foot of the cliff up to the cave entrance, where three cisterns of different shapes from the Roman period are visible. Pottery finds suggest that the cave was a place of cult in Hellenistic and Roman times. At several points inside, the walls are covered with clearly readable **ancient names and inscriptions** which date predominantly from the 4th century BC, some written in a natural iron-oxide pigment and others etched into an applied 'plaster'. The inscriptions are often of an erotic nature; some have interpreted this as relating to a phallic cult of initiation into manhood, which was practised in the cave by the *ephebes* of the island, and which may have been prompted by the phallic forms of stalactites within the chambers of the interior.

EAST & SOUTH OF CHORA

To the east of Chora the road leads down off the central
plateau through an arid rocky ravine to the island's only
port, **Karavostásis** (3km), on the east coast. This natural
harbour has always been the island's only point of con-
tact with the outside world: invaders—be they Ottomans,
or Russians in the 18th century, or Germans during the
Second World War—have always landed here. Furthermore, surface finds of pottery just to the north in the
area of Pountaki show that this area has been inhabited
since the 2nd millennium BC. The shoreline road to the
south of the harbour leads past several attractive beaches
to the sheltered, rural settlement of **Livádi** which is set
in a shallow rocky valley with wide views of Sikinos and
Ios. 'Livádi' means a meadow: the area has good wells and
constitutes one of the few low-lying fertile areas on the
island, although it is now virtually abandoned. Of interest
is the church of **Aghios Módestos**, to the right and above
the road as it turns in from the shore. The dedication to
Aghios Módestos—a 7th century saint who is the patron
of domestic animals and stock-breeders (as can be clearly
seen from the icons inside the church)—suggests that this
was the principal agricultural area of the island. There are
two parts of the church: an original chapel dating proba-

bly from the 13th century, with a subsequent church from a century later erected along its north side.

Due south of Chora, at a distance of 3.5km (*40 mins by foot*), is the unassuming **monastery-church of Aghios Nikolaos** (1.5km west of Petoúsis) whose buildings date from the late 16th century. It appears to occupy the site of an earlier Palaeochristian or pagan structure, fragments of which have been incorporated into its entrance and walls. The two (formerly three) contiguous chapels constitute most of the rectangular complex, leaving just sufficient space for cells, some stalls for animals and a threshing-floor.

WEST OF CHORA

Two hundred and fifty metres west of Chora, the road drops into a short dip: to the south at this point, just above the road, is the church of **Aghios Giorgios**. Above its west door the carved fragment of a pagan **grave-*stele***, depicting a figure on a charging horse with cape flying, has been immured in honour of the equestrian saint. The road then climbs onto a central ridge of the island, with a 220° panorama of the neighbouring islands—from Santorini in the southeast, through Sikinos, Ios, Naxos, Paros, Antiparos, Siphnos, Seriphos and Kimolos, to Milos in the west. To the south after 3km, a road branches steeply down to the cove and sheltered sandy beach at **Angáli** in Vathy Bay. This is one of the most protected spots on the island when the summer *meltemi* winds are in full force.

The western end of the island consists of the largely agricultural area of **Ano Meriá**, where grain is still harvested by hand and the fields ploughed with animals. The land has been cultivated here throughout history—as the scale and extent of the terracing show—but permanent habitation only began a little over a century ago, when it first became safe to leave the confines of the Chora and settle on this windswept plateau. For this reason Ano Meriá is a loose network of groupings of houses which extends for several kilometres. The traditional type of house here is a miniature independent complex, with storage areas, a living space, cistern, bread oven, chicken-coop, livestock-shelters and threshing floor, all closely packed around a central space so as to minimise the impact of the wind. Some idea of its furnishings, both domestic and agricultural, can be had from the small **Folklore Museum**, which stands to the south of the main road. (*Generally open July and Aug 5–10pm, otherwise T. 22860 41370.*) The museum building itself is whitewashed, but the surrounding buildings in un-rendered, dry-stone construction show the skill of the masons and the beauty of their craftsmanship.

At the western end of Ano Meriá (c. 6km from Chora, and 300m before the road to the western extremity of the island begins), a track branches south to the village's cemetery, descending past the church of **Aghios Ioannis Pródromos**—a low, barrel-vaulted structure of the 15th century with a large transverse narthex at its west end. Several patches of damaged wall-painting, dating from the 17th century or later, have been revealed from under the plaster on the south wall and the side of the vault. Further to the west, the main road (now a track) ends at the church of the Zoödochos Pigi which sits in an attractive and panoramic site below a large outcrop of rock crowned by an improvised, mediaeval watch-tower. From this eminence, **Cape Kastéllos**, the northernmost point of the island, can be seen. (*This is best approached via Aghios Giorgios Bay, which is reached in 40 mins by a stone mule-path, branching off to the north of the main track, from a point c. 500m before the church of the Zoödochos Pigi.*) On the ledge to the west of the bay of Aghios Giorgios, the site of an **Early Cycladic settlement** of the mid-3rd millennium BC, which has been partially revealed in excavations, can be seen: the visible walls probably date from a later occupation. This is the closest point of Folégandros to the island-group of Milos, Poliaigos and Kimolos, which are visible to the west. The settlement at Kastellos

must be related to the important, Early Cycladic centres
on Milos—even though the exposed crossing between
the two islands must have been hazardous for the sail-less
boats of the Early Bronze Age during the greater part of
the year.

PRACTICAL INFORMATION

840 11 Folégandros: area 32 sq.km; perimeter 42km; resident population 676; max. altitude 416m. **Port Authority**: T. 22860 41249. **Information**: Maraki Travel, T. 22860 41273 & 41221, www.folegandros. com

ACCESS

To reach Folégandros, it is often necessary to change ferries at Ios or Santorini. Direct connections to Athens are only twice weekly with *G.A. Ferries* (from Piraeus), and once a week with *NEL Lines* (from Lavrion). Throughout the summer however, there are frequent connections to Ios and Santorini, daily by fast Flying Dolphin or by regular ferry (*SAOS Lines*) five times weekly, which plies between Santorini and Ios, via Folegandros and Sikinos. This last is generally operated with the *F/B Arsinoe*—one of the museum-pieces of Greek ferry lines, with a small chapel dedicated to St Nicholas, patron of mariners, on its upper deck.

LODGING

Small and characterful, the most pleasant hotel on Folégrandros is the *Kastro Hotel in the heart of the old Kastro,

with raftered rooms, traditional furniture and beautiful
views (*open Apr–Oct, T./fax.
22860 41230, www.hotel-
castro.com*). **Anemomilos
Studios** (*T. 22860 41309*) and
Artemis Rooms (*T. 22860
41313*), both at the beginning
of the road up to the church
of the Panaghia, are simpler,
but pleasant and panoramic.

EATING

Taverna Mimis in Ano Meriá,
4km from the chora, is a
traditional taverna, with a
number local dishes such as
rabbit with *matsata*—a home-
made pasta. The tavernas in
Chora aim more for tourists,
though **Spitikó** serves good
home-made dishes, as its
name implies.

GLOSSARY OF CLASSICAL, BYZANTINE & GREEK TERMS

aedicule—a niche, or small shrine, often with architectural frame

aghiasma—a place where there is holy water; a holy spring

agora—a large public space, mainly given over to commerce

anthemion—a decoration with a flower- or palmette-based design, often placed on the pinnacle of a pediment

Archaic period—the 7th and 6th centuries BC

arcosolium—the arched recess (often decorated) above a sarcophagus or place of burial in a catacomb

bifora—a window divided into two arched lights, divided by a column or mullion

brecciated—(a marble) shot through with angular fragments of rock or mineral, giving rise to large patches ('*breccie*') of different colour

catholicon—the church at the centre of an Orthodox monastery

dentils—the cut, rectangular, teeth-like decorations on

the underside of a cornice

di-style—possessing two columns supporting the (centre of the) portico

dromos—an entrance passage or axial approach to a tomb or building

ephebe—a boy in Greek society who had reached the age of puberty

exedra—an architectural protrusion or a free-standing structure of semicircular form

'**free-cross plan**'—design of a church in which the lateral arms protrude freely from the body of the building (cp. 'inscribed cross plan' below)

Geometric period—the 10th-late 8th centuries BC

Hellenistic period—era of, and after, the campaigns of Alexander the Great, c. 330–c. 150 BC

heroön—a monument or building (generally circular) which commemorates a hero or mythical person

iconostasis—the high wooden screen (generally holding icons and images) which separates the sanctuary from the main body of an Orthodox church, and which with time came to substitute the masonry templon (*see below*) of earlier Byzantine churches

in antis—(of columns) set between projecting side-walls or wings (*antae*) of a building

'**inscribed cross plan**' or '**cross-in-square**'—design of a church whose exterior is square, but within which the interior space is articulated in the shape of a cross

isodomic—(of masonry) constructed in parallel courses of neatly-cut rectangular blocks

kalderimi—a stone-paved or cobbled pathway or mule-track

kambos—any fertile area near a settlement used for food-cultivation

Mani—a region of mainland Greece occupying the central, south-projecting promontory of the Peloponnese, to the south of Mount Taygetos

naos—the central interior area of a Byzantine church or the inside chamber of a pagan temple

parecclesion—a discrete chapel attached and parallel to a larger main church

peribolos—the perimeter wall of a temple precinct

phialostomia—hollow terracotta tubes or mouths with crimped sides, immured in the masonry of Byzantine buildings for decorative purposes and to ventilate the walls

pithos (pl. *pithoi*)—a large, tall, ceramic storage jar, sometimes used also for burials

'**poros' stone**—any soft limestone of porous composition used for construction

spolia—elements and fragments from ancient buildings

re-used in later constructions

stele (pl. *stelai*)—a carved tablet or grave-stone

synthronon—the rising, concentric rings of seats for the clergy in the apse of a church

Taxiarchis (pl. *Taxiarches*)—Archangel

templon—the stone or masonry screen in a church which closes off the sanctuary

trabeation—the upper part of an ancient building above the columns (including the architrave, frieze, cornice, etc.)

INDEX

General

Alexios I Comnenus	32
Al-Idrisi	109
Barbarossa	13, 63
Bent, Theodore	88, 95, 96, 107
Buondelmonti, Cristoforo	109
Elytis, Odysseas	63, 93
Gaitis, Yiannis	63, 71
Ghisi family	12, 13, 27
Gozzadini family	109, 110
Homer	59, 62, 73–76
Kaparias, Konstantinos	116
Le Corbusier	9, 31
Pasch van Krienen, Count	76, 88
Pausanias	62, 73, 74, 75
Pitton de Tournefort, Joseph	31, 36
Pliny	62, 73
Protopsaltis, Dionysios	94
Ross, Ludwig	88, 97
Sanudo, Marco	12, 62, 88, 109
Semonides	11
Solon	87
Strabo	62, 73, 109

Amorgos   **9–57**
  Aegiale, Ancient   49–50
  Aghia Thekla   25
  Aghia Triada, church of, Langáda   51
  Aghii Anargyri, church of the, Katapola   16
  Aghii Anargyri, church of the, Tholaria   50
  Aghii Saranda, church of the   25
  Aghios Giorgios Varsamítis, monastery of   35–36
  Aghios Ioannis Apokephalistís, church of   39
  Aghios Ioannis Chrysóstomos, church of   34–35
  Aghios Ioannis, church of, Lefkés   25
  Aghios Ioannis Pródromos, church of   50
  Aghios Ioannis Theologos, Káto Kámbos   45
  Aghios Ioannis Theologos, monastery of   52–53
  Aghios Nikolaos, church of   47
  Aghios Nikolaos, church of, Kamari   38
  Aigiáli   48
  Apáno Potamós   51
  Archaeology Museum   28–29
  Arkesine, Ancient   39–40
  Arkesíni   40
  Asfondilítis   47
  Astratios   50
  Chora   27–30
  Chozoviótissa, monastery of the   30–35

Amorgos continued

Christós Photodótis, monastery of	30
Dokathismata	38
Early Christian basilica, Káto Kámbos	45
Early Christian chapel, Paradísa	44
Evangelismós, church of the, Nerá	17
Hellenistic tower, Aghia Triada	41–43
Hellenistic tower, Ríchti	46–47
Kastro	27
Katapola	14–16
Káto Kámbos Bay	45
Káto Meriá plateau	40
Káto Potamós	51
Kinaros, islet	53
Kórax, Mount	43
Koutelós, Mount	49
Krambousa, islet	44
Kroúkelos, Mount	13, 53–54
Kyra [E]Leousa, church of the	27–28
Langáda	51
Levitha, islet	53
Lefkés	25
Markianí	37–38
Minoa, Ancient	20–25
Mycenaean cemetery, Nerá	17

Amorgos continued

Nikouriá, islet   46, 47–48, 51, 54

Panaghia, chapel of the, Katapola   16

Panaghia Epanochorianí, church of the   50

Panaghia Katapolianí, church of the   15–16

Panaghia Theoskepastí, chapel of   35

Panaghia tou Polití, church of the, Kolophána   44

Paradísa, bay of   44

Pramatevtís, Mount   53

Prophitis Elias, Mount   34

Pyrgí   43

Rachídi   16, 20

Stavrós   36–37

Stavros, church of the   53

Stroumbos   51

Tholaria   49, 50

Vroútsi   39

Xylokeratídi   16–17

Ios   **59–82**

Aghia Ekaterini, church of   68

Aghia Irini, church of, Ormos   64

Aghia Theodóti   76–77

Aghios Andreas and Aghia Kyriakí, church of   69

Ios continued

Aghios Giorgios, church of, Chora   69

Aghios Giorgios, church of, Ormos   64

Aghios Ioannis Prodromos, church of, Chora   68

Aghios Ioannis Prodromos, monastery of   80

Aghios Nikolaos, church of, Psáthi   79

Archaeological Museum   67–68

Chora   66–70

Epano Kambos   71–72

Frangokklisía, church of   69

Gaitis-Simosi Museum, Mylopótas   71

Hellenistic farmstead, Epano Kambos   72

Manganári, bay of   80

Mylopótas   70–71

Ormos Bay   63–64

Palaiokastro   78

Panaghia Kremniótissa, church of the   69

Panaghia Palaiokastrítissa, Palaiokastro   78

Psaropyrgos watchtower   72–73

Psáthi   76, 78–79

Pyrgos, monastery of   77–78

Skarkos   64–66

Tomb of Homer   73

Yialos   64

Sikinos   **85–104**
  Aghios Giorgios Avlaki   100
  Aghios Nikolaos, church of, Aloprónia   90
  Aghios Stephanos, church of   93
  Aloprónia   89–90
  Bonamá, spring of   89
  Byzantine Museum   92
  Chorió (Chora)   91–94
  Episkopí, church of the   95–99
  Folklore Museum   93
  Kastro   91–92
  Metamorphosis, church of the   94–95
  Palaiokastro   100–102
  Panaghia Pantanassa, church of the   92
  Panaghia 'Sykia', church of the   89–90
  Sikinos, Ancient   95, 99
  Troullos, Mount   95
  Zoödochos Pigi, monastery of the   93–94

Folégandros   **107–124**
  Aghia Sophia   113
  Aghios Antonios, church of   114
  Aghios Giorgios, church of   119
  Aghios Ioannis Pródromos, church of   121
  Aghios Módestos, church of, Livádi   118–119

Folégandros continued

Aghios Nikolaos, church of, Chora 112–113
Aghios Nikolaos, monastery-church of 119
Angáli 120
Ano Meriá 120
Cape Kastéllos 121
Chora 110–117
Chrysospiliá, cave of 117
Early Cycladic settlement 121–122
Folklore Museum, Ano Meriá 120
Karavostásis 118
Kastro 113–114
Livádi 118
Palaiokástro 116–117
Panaghia, church of the 115–116
Panaghia Eleousa, church of the 114
Panaghia Pantanassa, church of the 114
Panaghia Theoskepastí, church of the 114
Piatsa 114
Plateia Dounavi 112
Plateia Kontarini 114
Plateia Pounta 112
Taxiarch, church of the 113

Nigel McGilchrist is an art historian who has lived in the Mediterranean—Italy, Greece and Turkey—for over 30 years, working for a period for the Italian Ministry of Arts and then for six years as Director of the Anglo-Italian Institute in Rome. He has taught at the University of Rome, for the University of Massachusetts, and was for seven years Dean of European Studies for a consortium of American universities. He lectures widely in art and archaeology at museums and institutions in Europe and the United States, and lives near Orvieto.